P9-CAM-095

HISTORY LIVES
VOLUME ONE

PERIL

AND

PEACE

CHRONICLES OF

THE ANCIENT CHURCH

HISTORY LIVES
VOLUME ONE

PERIL
AND PEACE

CHRONICLES OF
THE ANCIENT CHURCH

MINDY AND
BRANDON WITHROW

CF4·K

10 9 8 7 6 5 4 3
This edition © copyright 2005 Mindy and Brandon Withrow
Christian Focus Publications
Reprinted 2007, 2009, 2010
ISBN: 978-1-84550-082-5

Published by Christian Focus Publications,
Geanies House, Fearn, Tain, Ross-shire,
IV20 1TW, Scotland, U.K..
www.christianfocus.com
email:info@christianfocus.com

Cover design by Jonathan Williams
Cover illustration by Jonathan Williams
Printed and bound in Denmark
by Norhaven A/S

For Eilidh,
Eoin,
Máire
and Aine

May you be God's gladiators,
with helmets of faith and spears of love.

C⊕NTENTS

Ancient Church Timeline
3 BC-590 AD

Note: "c." stands for circa, *a Latin word meaning "around or about."*

3-4 BC	Jesus is born
30-33 AD	Jesus dies and is resurrected
34	Paul is converted on Damascus road
46	Paul begins his missionary journeys
64	Rome burns; persecution under Nero begins
64, 67	Peter and Paul are martyred under Nero
70	Jerusalem is destroyed by Titus
79	The volcano Mount Vesuvius destroys Pompeii
80	Colosseum in Rome is completed
81-96	Domitian persecutes the church
98-117	Persecution under Trajan
110	Ignatius is martyred
118	Rome's population exceeds 1 million
138-161	Persecution under Antonius Pius
155	Polycarp is martyred
c.160	Tertullian is born
165	Justin is martyred
177	Marcus Aurelius begins his reign
180	Greek doctor Galen makes important discoveries about the heart and brain
c. 200	Origen founds his school in Alexandria
250	Persecution under Decius begins
258	Cyprian is martyred
276	Mani, leader of the Manicheans, is executed
284	Persecution under Diocletian begins

285	Diocletian divides empire into East and West
c. 300	Parchment replaces papyrus as standard writing material; library in Alexandria reaches 500,000 volumes
312	Constantine conquers Rome and reunites empire
313	Edict of Milan
315	Arian controversy begins
325	Council of Nicea
328	Athanasius becomes Bishop of Alexandria
329	Gregory Nazianzus is born
347	John Chrysostom is born
362	Emperor Julian reinstates paganism
370	Basil the Great becomes Bishop of Caesarea
372	Books replace scrolls
381	Council of Constantinople
390	Ambrose defies Emperor Theodosius
391	Library in Alexandria is destroyed
395	Roman Empire divided again after death of Theodosius
398	Council of Carthage
405	Jerome publishes his final installment of the *Vulgate*
410	Rome is conquered by Alaric I
413	Augustine begins writing *City of God*
430	Patrick becomes missionary to Ireland
431	Council of Ephesus
433	Attila the Hun attacks the Roman Empire
451	Council of Chalcedon
476	Roman Empire captured by the Franks
529	Benedict founds monastery at Monte Cassino
537	King Arthur dies
541	Bubonic Plague devastates Europe
549	Totila captures Rome
570	Mohammed, founder of Islam, is born
590	Gregory the Great becomes the first pope; beginning of the medieval church

What was the Ancient Church?

AFTER JESUS ASCENDED into heaven (in 30 or 33 AD), he sent the Holy Spirit to guide his apostles. Through these men, Jesus established his church. The apostles wrote the books of the New Testament and started churches throughout the Roman Empire. When the last apostle, John, died around 90 AD, the work of the apostles was carried on in the ancient church by the *church fathers*.

The earliest of the church fathers were friends of the apostles. One of the first fathers is Papias, a student of the Apostle John. Other church fathers like Ignatius of Antioch and Clement of Rome also lived during John's lifetime and may have known some of the apostles. Many of the letters and books these fathers wrote still exist, and these writings help us understand the life and beliefs of the early Christians.

As Christianity spread throughout the world, the church developed different kinds of officers to perform various tasks. A *deacon* collected offerings, cared for the poor and sick, and helped serve communion. A *presbyter* cared for the spiritual needs of a particular congregation, preaching, teaching, and baptizing. A *bishop* also preached, trained presbyters, supervised all the churches in a particular city, and represented his city at church councils. An *abbot* was a presbyter who led the congregation of a monastery, or abbey.

Some of the early Christians wrote books to defend Christianity against attacks from other religions. These writers, like Justin the Martyr, were called *apologists*. Their books are some of the earliest Christian writings. Most of them were written during the years of persecution. Some of these books were even addressed to Roman emperors, in an attempt to convince them to stop persecuting Christians.

Persecution continued for the first 300 years of the church, until Emperor Constantine declared Christianity a legal religion. Christians then became free to worship publicly. Without persecution, Christianity spread quickly throughout the empire. But so did false teaching that claimed to be Christian.

When false teachers, or *heretics*, taught ideas contrary to God's Word, the fathers corrected them. If the false teaching became a common problem within the church, the fathers would gather together to make church-wide decisions. They traveled from their local cities to hold *councils*. These councils influenced how we understand the Bible today, and they tell us that early Christians were united in their beliefs.

The most famous heretics were the *Arians*, who rejected the teaching that Jesus is God. Those who defended the truth became known as the *orthodox*. Some of the emperors after Constantine were Arian, and some were orthodox. When an Arian emperor was on the throne, the orthodox Christians, and especially the bishops, sometimes had to flee for their lives. For over fifty years, the official policy of the Roman Empire switched back and forth from orthodox to Arian, depending on what the emperor believed. More lives were lost during those years of conflict. But the orthodox persisted in resisting the Arians until their ideas were officially declared unbiblical at the Council of Constantinople in 381 AD.

Some of the fathers believed that the more popular Christianity became in the empire, the more the truth was compromised. They felt that many Christians had lost the physical and mental discipline to serve Christ. To keep themselves from being corrupted by the world, they formed societies, called *monasteries*, outside of normal city life. The *monks* spent their mornings in prayer and their afternoons working in the fields or hand-copying the Bible or other books. Most of what we know about the ancient church is from the books they preserved by copying.

Men and women lived in separate monasteries. We sometimes picture these monks as hermits who never left their prayer cells, but monasteries were actually busy places. Here, the monks fed the poor, cared for sick people, and provided food and shelter for travelers on the road. They were places for Bible teachers to meet and talk about Scripture. Monks even traveled distances to preach the gospel in other regions.

Monasteries became more common after the Roman Empire was defeated by Gothic invaders. The life of the last church father, Gregory the Great, who was born in 540 AD, marks the beginning of a new period in church history known as the medieval church.

We often ignore the ancient church because they seem different. Some of their ideas are foreign to us. But despite the differences, the earliest Christians have much in common with us today. Like the church fathers, we preach the gospel, feed the poor, and build hospitals. Like the fathers, modern Christians around the world are persecuted and murdered because of their faith. The perils of false teaching, sin, and evil rulers are part of our Christian heritage.

The lives of the earliest Christians are marked by love, pain, peace, war, and death. Like gladiators, they entered the arena and faced swords, wild beasts, and fire. These Christians preserved the message of Jesus' salvation and passed it on to us so we could tell others. They are the roots of our family tree of faith.

PAUL: A SERVANT OF THE TRUE GOD

59 AD. THE ADRIATIC SEA, OFF THE ISLAND COAST OF MALTA.

THE SEA SURGED, and a wall of foamy water forced him below the surface. He thrust his head above the waves, sputtering for air in the driving rain. "It's not that far. Almost there," he told himself. He'd have reached the shore by now if the surf didn't keep pushing him under. Another swell broke over him, dragging him toward the beach. He stopped struggling and held his breath, letting the furious water propel him forward. When the foam drained away, he was left behind on the sandy strip, exhausted, his tunic twisted around his legs. He coughed up seawater. "This is how the prophet Jonah felt when he was vomited up by the fish," he thought.

Something hard pressed into the small of his back. He rolled over and clawed at the wet sand. It was a bowl from the ship's galley. He tossed it aside and sat up.

"Paul!"

Turning in the direction of the shout, he saw dozens of men climbing out of the water or picking themselves up from the beach, still clutching debris from the wreckage. Running against the rain, two men came across the beach toward him, waving their arms and yelling.

"Paul! You're alive!"

They pulled him to his feet.

"I told you we were going to make it," he said, brushing shells from his beard.

"Can't say the same thing about the ship."

Turning, he squinted through the dark raindrops at the churning Adriatic Sea. The ship's bow was stuck fast where it had run aground on the reef, and the pounding surf had finally carried away the splintered stern. They had thrown the mast and sail overboard in a final attempt to right the ship. Now, missing her tackle, the carved swan head at the prow slowly disappearing beneath the waves, she looked like a wounded sea monster sinking proudly to her final resting-place.

"I am sorry that I didn't take your advice."

Paul turned to the muscular man behind him. He had lost his helmet, and rain dripped down his nose and armor, but the centurion was clearly still in charge.

"We never should have left Crete in the stormy season, but the captain assured me he had good reasons to avoid wintering in that harbor."

Paul waved the apology aside. "Julius, if I had to choose between an experienced sea captain and a prisoner under my guard, I would have made the same decision. Where is the captain?"

Julius peeled a strand of seaweed off his sword. "He's rounding up his sailors. My men are gathering the rest of the imperial prisoners. Including you and your two slaves here, it looks like all 276 of us are present and accounted for."

"I know it's hard to believe, Julian, but I told you yesterday that this is exactly what the angel promised when he appeared to me. We would run aground on an island, he said, but no lives would be lost."

"Well, next time an angel appears to you on a sinking ship, I'll listen to you! My troops wanted to kill all of you to keep you from escaping, but I vowed to get you to Rome safely for your trial before the emperor."

A soldier approached with word that all the passengers had been pulled from the water and were assembled just beyond the beach. "Apparently we're on the island of Malta, sir," he reported. "The sailors didn't recognize it earlier because of the storm. Some of the natives spotted the ship and have come out to help us."

"The gods be praised," Julius said, attempting to shield his face from the rain. "Let's find some shelter on this rock."

With the two slaves behind him, Paul followed Julius to the waiting troops. Next to the tall, broad centurion, the bow-legged prisoner was short, his shoulders slightly hunched from repeated beatings. He tried to wipe the rain from his head, but his cloak was soggy and he succeeded only in smearing wet sand across his bald spot.

The natives were eager to show hospitality. "There are too many of you to stay in the village," said a young man, "but I, Symeon, can take you to a large cave that will get you out of the rain. This way."

The tattered band moved inland. At a rocky outcropping, Symeon located the entrance to a cave. It was dark and stale inside, but dry. They started a bonfire, and spread their clothes out on rocks to dry in the warmth.

"We're going to run out of dry wood before we drive the chill out of all these men," Paul said. "I'll go and see what else I can find." He nodded to Julius and went out to the mouth of the cave.

The rain had slowed to a drizzle. The little sunlight they had seen that day was fading and the air was turning colder. He collected a smattering of dead brush. "It's wet, but it might burn," he thought. As he carried it in to the fire, he felt a sharp pain in his wrist.

With a cry, he dropped the bundle into the fire, and a puff of smoke curled around him. A viper dangled from his arm, its fangs sunk deep in his skin.

The men leaped back in alarm.

Paul shook his hand violently, wrenching the snake loose. It fell into the fire with a hiss and the sudden stench of burning flesh.

"Paul!" One of his slaves rushed to his side. "Let me look at it."

"No, Luke, it's fine." He shook his hand again, wincing from the pain.

Symeon stepped forward with a trembling finger pointed at Paul. "You must be a murderer! You thought you had escaped your punishment at sea, but justice is making sure you die for your sins!"

Julius rose anxiously. "Paul, I haven't gone to all this trouble of providing you with safe passage to Rome for you to die on the way there!"

"I'm not going to die."

"Paul, let me see," insisted Luke.

Julius stopped pacing and waved Luke away. "What does a slave know about snakebites?"

"I'm not a slave. I'm a doctor."

Julius looked up sharply. "What do you mean you're a doctor?"

Luke pulled Paul into the circle of firelight and examined the two red slits in his wrist. "I just pretended to be his slave so you would let me travel with Paul." He pointed to their other companion, who was biting his lip. "Aristarchus isn't a slave either."

The centurion raised an eyebrow. "You tricked me? I'm impressed. How can an educated doctor be convincing as a slave?"

Luke shrugged, more concerned about Paul's wound than his

secret. "I had to do it. Paul is my patient, and my dearest friend."

"A breach of protocol," Julius declared. "But I suppose there is nothing I can do about it now."

"I don't think it matters," said Symeon. "Paul is about to die. No one survives the bite of that viper."

"His arm isn't swelling," Luke said. "I think he's going to be fine."

Around the circle, the men eyed him in silence. Nothing happened.

"Perhaps he is a sorcerer," murmured the natives. "It is a miracle he is not dead yet!"

"Paul has been involved in lots of miracles," said Aristarchus. "Tell them, Luke."

"It's true. Paul healed a crippled man in Lystra."

"And was almost stoned to death as his reward!" prompted Aristarchus.

Luke squatted next to Paul. "He cast a demon out of a slave girl in Philippi. Her angry master had him thrown in prison. Then an earthquake opened the prison gates, and Paul kept the jailer from committing suicide."

"And in Troas," added Aristarchus, "Paul preached someone to death! He had been preaching for hours and Eutychus fell asleep in a third-story window and fell to his death. Paul brought him back from the dead."

"He withstands the viper's bite and performs miracles!" exclaimed Symeon, wide-eyed. "Paul is a god!"

"No, no!" Paul insisted quickly. "I'm not a god, but a servant of the true God. It is because of his power that I performed those miracles."

"It's because of your god that you were arrested!" shouted one of the prisoners.

Symeon ignored the chuckling that followed that statement and cocked his head at Paul. "Why did your god have you arrested?"

Paul shifted into a more comfortable position on the rocky ground. "About thirty years ago, a Jew named Jesus was executed in Jerusalem for claiming to be God, blasphemy in the Jewish religion. He called himself the Way, the Truth, and the Life. After his death, Jesus' followers began to spread this religion of the Way. The Jewish religious leaders who had crucified Jesus went after his disciples."

"You were one of his disciples?"

Paul shook his head. "No, I was one of the religious leaders who opposed them. I worked tirelessly to round up everyone in Jerusalem who followed the Way and put them in jail. When I heard that these teachings had spread north into Damascus, I got permission to arrest the heretics there, too, and bring them back to Jerusalem. But instead of wiping out the Way in Damascus, something unexpected happened."

"What happened? Please, Paul, it is still raining and night has fallen. We have time for your story."

The men had stretched out across the cavern floor, the soldiers keeping a casual eye on the prisoners. Paul leaned forward and spread his hands out over the fire. The flickering shadows exaggerated his hooked nose and ran his eyebrows into a solid furrow. "That was back when I went by my Hebrew name Saul," he explained. "It's a long story."

"Yes, and I think you should rest right now," interrupted Luke. He turned to Symeon. "Paul will talk until this cave runs out of air. Perhaps I should tell the story."

Paul sat back and chuckled. "Luke is a better storyteller than I am anyway. He remembers every important detail."

"Well," Luke began, "as Paul said, it is a long story, and it takes place far from here . . ."

Luke went on to recount Paul's adventures... of course, at that time, Paul had not been his name. Saul and his fellow travelers had followed the road along the Sea of Galilee, crossing over the Jordan River north of the sea. Approaching a ridge about 12 miles south of Damascus, the city came into view below them. In the hot sun, the pale walls shimmered on the horizon. It was a welcome sight for the dirty, weary travelers.

"By nightfall, we'll be inside those gates," said one. "I can't wait to wash my tired feet!"

They were starting their descent when there was a sudden flash of light. It was white-hot, like the brightest bolt of lightning, and the travelers dropped to the ground in terror.

Ears ringing, the leader lay face down in the dust, arms over his head. He felt the earth vibrate with a deep growl that started far below him and gathered strength as it rushed toward the trembling surface.

"Saul! Saul!" boomed a terrible voice. In the desert he had once heard a wounded lion make a sound like that.

"Saul! Why do you persecute me?"

Squeezing his eyes shut, he fought back the panic. He tried to speak, but he had no voice.

"Wh—who are you?" Pressing his face into the gravel, he cut his lip and tasted blood.

"I am Jesus, who you are persecuting."

He wasn't sure that his heart was still beating. He'd lost the feeling in his arms. His eyes still shut, he became aware of a presence. It seemed he was looking straight into someone's eyes, deep, powerful, full of love.

"Jesus! What do you want me to do, Lord?" he cried.

"Stand up on your feet!"

He struggled to rise, afraid to open his eyes, afraid to look away from the beautiful and terrible face before him.

"I have appeared to you for this purpose, to appoint you a servant and a witness to the things you have seen. I have delivered you from your people and from the Gentiles, to whom I am sending you to open their eyes. They will turn from darkness to light, and from the power of Satan to the power of God. They will receive forgiveness for sin and a place among those I have set apart."

"Yes, Lord!"

"Go into the city, and you will be told what to do."

The vision faded. Bright spots of color danced in the darkness. He couldn't open his eyes. Clawing at his face, he felt a ridge over his eyelids as though the skin had melted. He stumbled and fell to his knees. "Help me," he whispered to his companions. "Help me!"

"What was that?" they demanded. "Was it an earthquake? What's wrong with your eyes?"

"Take me to Damascus," was all he could say.

They left him at an inn on Straight Street. Sitting in the rented room alone with his blindness, he cried out to God. How could he have been so wrong? "Lord Jesus, forgive me! Show me what to do."

For three days he didn't eat or drink, though the innkeeper shoved food at him twice a day. "What's wrong with you?"

"I'm waiting for someone," he muttered.

On the third day of his blindness, he heard a strange voice at the inn door. Two sets of footsteps came toward his room. Kneeling on the floor, he turned his face toward the visitor as he entered.

"Brother Saul," said the voice, close to his face.

He smelled cabbage on the visitor's breath.

"I'm Ananias. Jesus who you saw on the road sent me here."

"You know Jesus?" Saul whispered.

"Give me your face." Cold, damp hands covered his eyes. "Now you will see again and be filled with the Holy Spirit."

His eyelids began to twitch, and he blinked, dropping scales in his lap. He was suddenly looking into the kind face of an old man.

"I can see," he said. "I can see! Thank you, sir. What do I do now?"

"You must be baptized," said Ananias, "but first——." He called for the innkeeper. "Get this man something to eat."

Listening to Luke's story, Symeon let out a deep breath. He hadn't realized he had been holding it. "That is amazing," he whispered. "What happened next?"

Luke shifted and glanced at the bite on Paul's arm. It still wasn't swollen.

"I did exactly what Jesus told me to do," Paul said. "Starting in Damascus, and then in Jerusalem, I declared that all should repent and turn to God. I preached all over the empire, making several extended journeys, and starting churches in every city. As I traveled, I wrote letters back to these churches to encourage them and correct their beliefs. That is why the Jews seized me in the temple in Jerusalem and tried to kill me."

"You changed sides."

"Yes, once I knew the truth. Since then I have been in constant danger, and even now, I'm on my way to defend my case before the emperor. But God has preserved me, and so I am still alive today to tell you that what Moses and the prophets spoke about has come true. Jesus suffered, died and then rose from the dead to proclaim truth to Jews and Gentiles."

Symeon looked at him with shining eyes. "Paul, you must come into the village and meet Governor Publius. His father is very sick. You must heal him!"

"We'll go at first light."

Julius cleared his throat. "If you don't mind, I think I'll go along," he said sarcastically.

"Oh, yes." Symeon turned to the centurion. "Publius will want to dine with the man in charge."

Luke rolled over and chuckled into his cloak.

The cavern grew quiet as they settled in for a few hours' rest. Outside, the rain stopped. A sliver of moon rose over the tranquil sea. There was nothing left of the storm but fragments of the ship scattered across the beach.

The Bible records Paul's shipwreck experience in Acts 27. No one knows for sure if Luke and Aristarchus posed as Paul's slaves, but we do know they were with Paul on his journey to Rome. Friends and family members were not allowed to accompany prisoners, but the wealthiest prisoners could bring slaves to tend to their needs. A famous prisoner like Paul, highly respected by the centurion, would have been expected to board the ship with a slave or two.

Paul and his companions spent three months on Malta, where he healed the governor's father and introduced many of the people to Jesus. When the storm season was over, they boarded another ship and finished their journey to Rome. Paul remained under house arrest there for over two years, preaching and writing letters to the churches. In 67 AD, he was beheaded by the mad Emperor Nero.

After his death, Paul's letters were circulated all over the empire. Soon Christians everywhere considered his writings the Word of God, with the same authority as the Old Testament.

TERRIBLE TRIALS AND PERSECUTIONS

PERSECUTION IS TREATING people cruelly because of what they believe. When people die because of persecution, they are called *martyrs*. Jesus was persecuted, and since then many of his followers have been persecuted and martyred, too.

Ancient Christians knew persecution well. In these early days of the church, many Roman emperors tried to stop the spread of Christianity by torturing and killing Christians. These persecutions are road markers in church history. Some of the earliest persecutions, like the stoning of Stephen in Acts 8, show us how faithful these Christians were to the truth of the gospel.

Why did the emperors persecute Christians? Sometimes it was just because they hated Jesus and the Christians who followed him. Other times, Christians were killed or tortured, not because they worshiped Christ, but because they would not also worship false gods. The Romans believed that their many gods made the empire rich and protected it. They were afraid that if the Christians offended these gods by not worshiping them, the gods might get angry at Rome and allow Rome's enemies to conquer the empire. Because Christians refused to worship these false gods, the Romans believed they were unpatriotic or, even worse, guilty of treason against the empire. So even though it wasn't illegal to worship Jesus, it was illegal to refuse to worship the other gods as well.

The persecutions started in Rome during the reign of Emperor Nero and continued for almost 300 years, with brief periods of peace in between. Some persecutions were limited to a few cities, while others spread across the entire empire. Sometimes the emperors were just enforcing bad laws. But other times the emperors tortured Christians for entertainment.

This was the case with Nero (reigned 54-68 AD), one of the most famous Roman emperors, who went insane. During his reign, the apostles Peter and Paul were martyred. He murdered his mother, brother, and two wives to make sure they couldn't take the empire away from him. When Rome burned down in 64, everyone suspected Nero of starting the fire. To avoid being blamed for it, Nero accused the Christians who lived there, and thousands of Christians died. Some were fed to wild dogs. Others were covered in oil, nailed to wood, and set on fire as torches to light the city streets. Nero's troubled mind led him to commit suicide when he was only thirty-two.

Domitian (reigned 81-96), like some of the other emperors, believed he was a god and considered it atheism and treason when Christians refused to worship him. During his persecution many Christians were killed or exiled.

Trajan (reigned 98-117) was in many ways a good ruler and enforced the laws, but this included the laws used against Christians. Christianity was becoming popular in the empire, and many people stopped worshiping the Roman gods. Trajan believed that without this worship Rome would face the wrath of the gods, so he made the people attend the pagan worship services. It was under Trajan's rule that the great bishop of Antioch, Ignatius, was condemned to death. One of the better things Trajan did was make the law a little easier on Christians. He ordered one of his governors, Pliny, to refuse anonymous accusations, and that policy cut down on the number of accusations against Christians. He also said that Pliny should not go looking for Christians to persecute, but that they should only be arrested if he ordered them to sacrifice to the gods and they refused.

Septimus Severus (reigned 193-211) applied the death penalty to Christians. Decius (reigned 249-251) required all citizens to prove they had sacrificed to the gods or face torture and death. Diocletian (reigned 284-305) and his successors ordered that Christians be removed from the military and tortured, and that their homes and churches be destroyed and their books burned.

Finally, the official persecution of the Roman Empire ended when Constantine the Great defeated his rival emperor Maxentius at the battle of the Milvian Bridge. Constantine issued the Edict of Milan in 313, which made it legal for Christians in the empire to worship Jesus alone.

But persecution did not end with the ancient church. In the years that followed, Christians were persecuted in other parts of the world, and even today thousands of Christians around the globe are mistreated and often face death.

Polycarp: Ground like wheat in the lion's teeth

100 AD. SMYRNA, IN ASIA MINOR.

TWO MEN STOOD in front of a house on a broad street in the northern area of the city. One had graying hair and a slight curve of the shoulders. The other was taller and younger.

"You have become a courageous disciple, Polycarp. The city of Smyrna is getting a fine bishop."

"I've had an excellent teacher," the young man said, embracing his friend. "Thank you for all that you've taught me. I'll miss our great conversations."

"We'll have them again," replied the older man. He buckled a tattered cloak across his shoulders and picked up the leather pack at his feet. "Be bold, and pray for wisdom. Since the deaths of the apostles, the world has become even more dangerous for Christians. But I know God has a special destiny for you. Good-bye, my friend."

"Good-bye, Ignatius. God be with you on your journey."

The new bishop watched his friend disappear toward Golden

Street. From his vantage point, with the hill of Deirman Tepe on his right, the neat grid of broad, paved streets sloped away toward the harbor. In a few minutes, Ignatius would be boarding one of the cargo ships anchored there.

With a sigh, Polycarp leaned against the doorway and thought of Ignatius. Most of his youth had been spent studying with Ignatius and the Apostle John, learning from them what it meant to follow Jesus. "John died in exile," he said to himself, "and Ignatius is going back to his church in Antioch. I have only God to guide me now." He took his friend's advice and asked God for wisdom.

Every Sunday at sunrise, the Christians of Smyrna gathered at the home of Polycarp's neighbor to worship. Titus had a large house, with numerous rooms opening off a central courtyard, but it wasn't big enough to hold everyone. Those who arrived last stood in an adjoining room and listened as Polycarp preached in the courtyard. They sang psalms together and prayed, and then celebrated the Lord's Supper.

Under Polycarp's leadership, the church grew.

"I'm going to sell some property, Bishop," Titus announced. "With the money, I can add a second courtyard to the house. We'll be able to fit 100 more people every Sunday."

"God bless you for your generosity!" Polycarp grinned. "Any chance we can add a fountain to use for baptisms?"

"Absolutely. But I don't think I will tell the builder what it is for. No need to get ourselves in trouble with the authorities."

As Ignatius had warned, it was becoming more and more dangerous to be a Christian. The Roman rulers believed in many gods, but the Christians would worship only one God.

"The Romans call us atheists since we won't worship their idols," Polycarp preached one Sunday in Titus's new courtyard. "They worship almost anything, even the River Meles! But because they reject the true God, they are the ones who are atheists."

After the service, a little girl came to him with a question. "Atheism is a crime, and criminals are fed to the wild beasts in the Colosseum." She raised large, honey-colored eyes to the bishop. "What will we do if we get arrested?"

He crouched down and put both hands on the girl's shoulders. "We will continue to do what we have always done," he said gently. "We will obey the commandments of Jesus and we will not worship the emperor or any other false god, no matter how they threaten us."

He sat at his desk that afternoon and thought of the stories John had told him about Peter and Paul and how they were killed at the hands of Emperor Nero. He thought of the recently completed Colosseum in Rome where criminals were taken to fight wild beasts for the entertainment of the people. "O God," he prayed silently, "change Emperor Trajan's heart and make him recognize you as king. If you call your people to face the lions in the stadium, give them the courage to stay true to you."

It was a pleasant afternoon, and the myrrh trees in the garden were pungent. Polycarp often prayed there, away from prying eyes, accompanied only by the nectar-seeking bees. Startled by rapid footsteps, he looked up from the corner where he knelt. A woman from his congregation reached for him with tears in her eyes.

"Tavia, what's wrong?"

"Ignatius has returned to Smyrna. He is staying at my house and has asked to see you."

He jumped up. "Ignatius is here? Why does that make you cry?"

"He has been arrested for atheism!"

"As I feared," he thought, squeezing his eyes shut. "Take me to him, please."

Soldiers with spears were posted at the door to the house, but when they recognized Tavia, they let them enter. Polycarp ran to his friend.

"Ignatius! What has happened?"

The years had changed his appearance. His face was wrinkled and his beard white, and he hunched over in his chair. But he looked happy.

"I have been tried for atheism, my friend," he said with a smile. "Emperor Trajan gave me the choice of worshiping him and denying Christ, or being sent to Rome to die. He would have killed me then, but there is a big feast in Rome and I am to join some lions in entertaining the people at the Colosseum."

"No, no!" Polycarp cried. "There must be something we can do."

Ignatius shook his white head and rested a hand on Polycarp's shoulder. "No, I want to do this. Don't try to rescue me. God has called me to die for him and I am ready. I am his wheat, and when I am ground by the lion's teeth I will become the pure bread of Christ."

A soldier jerked his head towards the door. "Time to go," he said. "The prisoner has a boat to catch."

Ignatius rose slowly, reaching for his walking stick. "Go, my friend, and be strong. God will give you courage. I will write to you if I can."

Polycarp stumbled out of the house. He was angry and afraid, but he knew his friend was right again. "Ignatius cannot deny Christ any more than the apostles could. Maybe Trajan will change his mind and let him go," he thought. He returned to the garden and prayed more urgently.

"Pray for your fellow believers like Ignatius," he preached that Sunday. His voice rang out across the marble tiles, echoing in the adjoining rooms. "Pray for the emperor and our local governors. Pray for your enemies and the enemies of Jesus. And pray for yourselves, that the lives you live will be evidence of your true faith in Christ."

Weeks passed. He continued to pray that Ignatius would have courage and that the emperor would become a Christian. One morning, a messenger delivered a letter.

That is Ignatius's handwriting! "Thank you," he said to the messenger. When the boy left, he unrolled the scroll with trembling hands.

My dear Polycarp, the letter read. *I have just left Troas, the last stop on my way to Rome. It looks as though I won't have time to finish writing to my friends, so would you please write to them for me? Tell them how much I have loved them and encourage them to be strong. When I think of the Colosseum, I pray that you will be God's gladiator. Let faith be your helmet and love be your spear, for where the battle is hard, the reward is greater. Good-bye in the name of Jesus.*

He rolled the letter and tucked it tenderly into his belt, the tears welling up in his eyes. The letter would have taken some weeks to arrive, so Ignatius was probably already dead. "Good-bye, my friend," he whispered. "Good-bye until I see you next in the heavenly city."

The church in Smyrna continued to grow despite the persecution. Polycarp became bolder in his preaching. Just as he had been a disciple of Ignatius, he took a young man named Irenaeus as his disciple.

As the years passed, the persecution became more intense.

One February day, it happened.

"Bishop! Come quickly!" Irenaeus burst into Polycarp's study.

He did not see as well as he used to, now that he was an old man, but it was clear from the worry on his disciple's face what had happened.

"Soldiers are on their way here," Irenaeus said. "The governor has ordered you to stand trial for atheism. You must hide."

Polycarp stood up slowly and shook his head. "They call me a criminal, but I will not act like one and try to escape."

"You know what happened to the others like Ignatius who were charged with atheism. You'll be killed in the blood games!"

"I'm not afraid of death. It would be a privilege to die for my Savior like Ignatius did."

But other friends arrived then and pleaded with him. "Please, Bishop. Allow us to take you away. Do it for us. What will we do without our teacher?"

"Very well," he agreed finally. "But I won't go far. I need to be close to my people in case there is a need."

They went out to the street. Hunching down in the back of a cart, he covered himself with an old blanket. The cart bounced along as Irenaeus led the way out of the city and into the countryside. The road followed the coast, and Polycarp could hear the waves of the Aegean Sea crashing against the cliffs. The blanket stank of horse sweat, and he lifted a corner of it and breathed in the sea air. Finally, they pulled up to a farmhouse in a grove of fig trees. Polycarp knew the owner.

"What's the matter?" Farmer Marcus asked when they arrived in haste. They told him of the attempted arrest.

"With God's help we will do all we can to protect you here. Come inside."

For several days, the bishop stayed with Marcus and his family, spending most of the time in prayer. On the third night there was a frantic knocking at the door. Polycarp sat up quickly in his bed.

"Shh!" Marcus whispered as he rushed to the door. "Stay around the corner until I find out who it is."

He cracked the door and lifted his candle to the opening. Irenaeus stood anxiously on the doorstep, with a horse and wagon behind him in the shadows.

"Bishop, come quickly," Irenaeus said, pushing his way in and taking Polycarp by the arm. "The soldiers have discovered your hiding place and are on their way here. I have a wagon to take you somewhere else where friends are waiting."

The three of them hurried outside. "Go, my friend," Marcus said, embracing Polycarp. "God be with you."

The night was cold. Polycarp pulled his thin cloak around him and painfully climbed up behind the crates in the wagon. With a crack of the whip, the horse broke into a gallop. As he huddled on the rattling floorboards, Polycarp prayed. "Protect Marcus, and the church members in the city. Change the emperor's heart. And, no matter what happens, give me the strength to be faithful to you."

He was still praying when they arrived at another farm. In the darkness, he stepped down into the welcoming arms of his friend Flavius. The horse and wagon rumbled away, disappearing into the night.

Flavius drew Polycarp into the house. "They will never find you here," he said. He motioned to a young slave. "Go, prepare a bed for our visitor."

But it was still dark when they heard the marching feet of a regiment of soldiers. "Search the property!" a voice ordered outside.

Flavius and Polycarp slipped out the back door and made their way to a shed away from the house. "Quick! Into the corner!" Flavius whispered.

Polycarp hunched in the shadows, trying to catch his breath. "Your will be done, Lord," he prayed silently.

The door flew open. Farming tools clanged to the floor as the soldier hastily searched the shed. "There's no one here, Sir!"

"On to the next farm then!" cried a voice as the door banged shut.

Polycarp and Flavius waited in the shed for nearly an hour to be sure the soldiers had gone. When they stepped outside, it was light. The sun had risen, and a flock of sheep waited near the gate to be let out for breakfast on the hillside.

A young man ran toward them as they returned to the house. "Sir," he said, wringing his hands. "The soldiers. They took him. They said they would make him help them."

Flavius put his head in his hands. "My slave boy," he said to Polycarp. "They'll torture him until he tells them you're here. I've failed you, friend. You will have to hide somewhere else."

"No," the bishop said firmly. "Running was a bad idea from the start. I will not let them hurt anyone else for me. I'll wait here until they return, and when they do, I'll go back to Smyrna and stand trial."

Flavius tried to persuade him to go, but Polycarp had made up his mind. He went into the house and rested until the soldiers returned.

It was almost time for the evening meal when he heard them arrive. They were already in the house when he went downstairs to meet them.

"Good evening, Captain," he said. "There is no need for violence. I will come with you willingly."

The captain was surprised. "This old man looks too frail to be a dangerous criminal," he thought. He put his sword away and turned to Polycarp. "Sir, you are under arrest," he said. "We've been ordered to take you to the governor."

"Yes, I know," Polycarp replied. "But it is time for dinner and your men look hungry. Please have something to eat and drink before we leave." He asked Flavius to bring out some food for the soldiers.

The captain hesitated.

Polycarp stepped closer. "Please allow your men to eat, Captain, and give me an hour to pray. Then I will go with you willingly."

"What harm can it do?" the captain thought. "Very well," he said. "One hour."

The soldiers reclined on couches around the table as bowls of fruit and bread were brought out. Polycarp began to pray aloud. The soldiers ate in silence, listening as the old man prayed for them, and the governor, and the emperor. He thanked God for the gift of Jesus and for his long life of serving him. He asked God to make him faithful in death and to keep his church faithful when he was gone.

The captain was amazed at the old man's courage. "It doesn't seem right to arrest a man like this," he thought.

It was two hours before Polycarp ended his prayer.

"He will ride in my carriage," the captain ordered his soldiers. "The rest of you will follow on foot." They headed back toward the city.

"There's no reason for a kind old man like you to die," the captain said when they were alone in the carriage. "The governor just wants you to deny that you're a Christian and offer a sacrifice to the emperor. Just do what he asks, and he'll let you go."

Polycarp sat quietly and looked out of the window at the passing fields.

"Listen to me," the captain insisted. "Religion is a silly thing to die for. You're an old man now! Just bow to the emperor's statue and save yourself."

Polycarp turned to the captain. "I appreciate your concern," he said firmly. "But I will not take your advice and deny my Lord."

"You're a silly old fool!" cried the captain angrily. "If you have such little care for your own life, then you can walk the rest of the way!" He threw open the carriage door and shoved Polycarp out.

Painfully, the bishop got to his feet. His shin was scraped and bleeding, but he ignored it and followed behind the carriage. For several miles he hobbled along, surrounded by foot soldiers, their metal armor clanking as they marched.

Finally, they came to the arena. Polycarp heard the crowd long before he saw them. The people filled the stands, drunk and shouting, waiting for the next show. Somewhere beneath the stands the animal cages reeked of dung. Polycarp waited in an entrance while the captain approached the governor in the stands.

When the captain turned, Polycarp gazed directly into his eyes and saw the soldier's regret. But it was too late.

Governor Quadratus called for the bishop to be brought forward. The crowd cheered and came to their feet as Polycarp was led onto the field. He noticed fresh blood soaking into the dirt where he stood.

"Are you Polycarp, the Christian teacher?" the governor asked.

"I am."

Quadratus leaned forward and spoke in a low voice. "Sir, have respect for your age. This is no place for an old man. Just tell them what they want to hear so I can let you go. Just say 'away with the atheists' and you can leave in peace."

Polycarp looked directly into the governor's eyes. "You want me to say 'away with the atheists'?" He turned and waved his hand over the bloodthirsty crowd. "These are the atheists," he said. "Away with the true atheists."

"I am trying to make this easy for you," Quadratus said, frowning. "Take the oath of allegiance to the emperor and I will let you go."

"My allegiance is not to the emperor, but to Christ," the old man replied. "For eighty-six years I have been the servant of Christ and he has done me no wrong. How can I deny the king who saved me?"

The governor pounded both fists on his knees. "Sir, don't put me in a difficult position! Say what I told you to say and we can end this show."

Polycarp drew back his stooped shoulders and held his head upright. "Apparently, sir, you don't understand me. Let me be very clear, so there can be no mistake." He raised his voice. "I am a Christian. If you want to know more about what I believe, name the day and I will explain my doctrine to you more fully."

Quadratus pointed to the noisy crowd. "Persuade the people to let me do so."

Polycarp smiled sadly. "You, Governor, are worthy of such an explanation. I can see that you really respect my position and want to understand my beliefs. But these people are not interested in respect or conviction."

"Why do you fight me?" Quadratus spat the words. "I have wild beasts, and I will deliver you to them if you do not change your mind!"

"Bring them in then. I was a sinner, but Christ saved me. Why would I want to go back to my sin?"

"If the lions don't scare you, perhaps fire will!" shouted the governor, coming to his feet. "I will have you burned at the stake unless you do as I say!"

"You threaten me with a fire that burns temporarily," Polycarp said quietly, "because you do not understand the fire of hell which will burn eternally and punish the wicked. Don't put this off any longer, Governor. Do what you are going to do."

Quadratus sank back into his chair and dropped his head into his hands. When he looked up again, he motioned carelessly to a guard. Walking out into the middle of the arena, the guard shouted, "Polycarp has confessed that he is a Christian!"

At this, the crowd came to their feet with a thunderous roar. "Feed him to the lions!" they cried. "Feed him to the wild beasts!"

Quadratus stood, and the people hushed. "The games have been closed for the day. I cannot release the lions."

A great uproar rose again from the crowd. "Then burn him! Burn the atheist!"

Quadratus looked again at Polycarp. The bishop's bearded face was calm and gentle, but the stubbornness behind the eyes told him the old man would never deny his God. Wearily, the governor nodded and dropped back into his seat.

With bloodthirsty screams, the crowd leaped over the stands and rushed out onto the field toward Polycarp. He knew this was the end, but he was not afraid. He closed his tired eyes. "Father, I praise you for my salvation," he prayed. In the middle of the screaming crowd, he took off his coat, then squatted down and removed his sandals.

From somewhere, dozens of sticks and branches were thrown into a pile on the arena floor. Several men from the crowd took a rope and tied Polycarp's hands behind his back. They were about to nail his hands to a wooden plank when he said, "There is no need to use nails. My God who gives me strength to endure the flames will give me the strength to stay in the flames without the security of your nails."

They shrugged and propped him up on the pile of wood. Before they could light the fire, he began to speak again. The mob quieted to hear his words.

"O Lord God Almighty," he prayed, "thank you for giving me the privilege of giving up my life for you today, and to share in the sufferings of Jesus on the cross. Thank you for your promise of eternal life for both my soul and my body. Today receive me as a sacrifice. I praise you for all things and glorify you now and forever through your son Jesus. Amen."

The crowd was silent for a moment until someone yelled, "Burn the Christian!" Then the whole crowd began to chant, "Burn the Christian! Burn the Christian!"

Someone brought a burning torch, and the pile of wood was set on fire.

The flames were hot. He remembered the words of Jesus, "Whoever wants to save his life will lose it, but whoever loses his life for my sake will find it." He remembered the words of his friend Ignatius, "Let faith be your helmet and love be your spear, for where the battle is hard, the reward is greater."

Polycarp closed his eyes and smiled. He knew he was about to meet Jesus and see his dear friend Ignatius once again.

Polycarp's martyrdom became one of the most famous stories of the ancient church, inspiring thousands of Christians in the years that followed to stay faithful to God in the midst of persecution. Only one of his writings has survived, an encouraging letter he wrote to the church in Philippi.

JUSTIN: A FLAME WAS KINDLED IN MY SOUL

165 AD. ROME.

SEVEN FIGURES STRODE along the narrow street. It was late afternoon, well past the hottest part of the day, and the orange sun shimmered low in the sky. Street vendors were packing their wares into carts and heading home or to the public baths. Many of the market stalls were already deserted, the racks that an hour ago displayed linens and pottery now empty.

"Justin, is this really safe?"

"How can one be any safer than in the hands of God, Chariton?" The speaker was a tall, slender man. His brown tunic, with a rectangular white mantle buckled around his shoulders, identified him like a uniform. It was a philosopher's garment, the sign of an educated man.

Chariton clapped his friend on the shoulder. "Always the optimist! That's why you're in charge. Still, this whole thing is a bit suspicious."

"Working in the emperor's palace gives me an advantage," said

43

Euelipistus. "I've asked around, but there are no rumors of action against Justin."

"Crescens is still sore from the last time you defeated him in a debate," said a fourth companion, walking backwards. Hierax threw a suspicious glance at two aristocrats who had paused behind them, talking in low voices.

"Crescens is a foul beast, no doubt about it," said Justin, "but I don't fear him."

A young man, little older than a boy, scampered between Justin and Hierax. "I'm not afraid either, Justin! I won't turn back."

"Ah, Paeon, remember the Apostle Peter," said the philosopher with a smile.

"What about him?"

"He, too, said he would never turn back, but he did."

"The only thing that makes me want to turn back," said Charito, the only woman among them, "is the horrible smell of that barbarian Crescens." She wrinkled her nose and tossed her head, shaking a knot of dark hair at the back of her neck.

A passing merchant dropped a crate of onions. Justin and Paeon paused to help him gather the scattered produce, then caught up with their friends. Liberianos lagged at the back of the group, staring vacantly and mumbling.

Paeon poked a finger at him. "What did you say?"

Liberianos blinked. "What?"

"It sounded like you said, 'Marcus Aurelius.'"

"I said that aloud? I guess I was thinking that after trying for so long to convince the emperors that Christians are not their enemies, it seems like Marcus Aurelius should have changed things."

"True," affirmed Chariton with a nod. "Marcus is the best philosopher to sit on the imperial throne. He's the one who says that all things should be done with kindness, freedom, dignity, and justice."

"He also congratulates anyone who is willing to give up his life for what he believes," added Euelipistus.

"Yes, he does," said Justin. "But he also thinks that Christians who give up their lives for Jesus are irrational and obstinate. I've written many books trying to convince people otherwise, but they prefer to listen to buffoons like Crescens. He still believes in the old Roman gods and argues that if we refuse to sacrifice to them, we are anti-Roman."

"Maybe after tonight he'll change his mind," Charito suggested.

"Anytime Crescens invites Justin to debate," said Hierax, scowling, "he certainly has something planned in his own favor."

The group arrived at the forum. The heart of the city, it was a broad, paved courtyard, with dozens of marble pillars supporting a flat roof. They had arrived early for the debate, but already a good many people had gathered.

Justin scanned the crowd, spotting Crescens leaning against a pillar. They had begun to make their way toward him when a slave ran up with a message for Justin. "Excuse me, Teacher. Crescens asks that you wait here briefly." He stood off to the side, eyes on the ground.

"Did he say why?"

"No, Teacher, just that he wanted you to wait."

Justin looked over at Crescens. He didn't budge from the pillar, except for an almost imperceptible nod to Justin.

"Why does he keep us from approaching?" asked Paeon.

"Because he's a glutton, a liar, and a lover of money," quipped Justin, "and if he is convicted of the truth, he'll have to give up all of them!"

They chuckled.

"What's going on over there?" said Hierax, as a murmur ran through the forum. The crowd parted abruptly, and a regiment of soldiers burst upon them, seizing Justin and his friends around the shoulders.

A punch from Paeon was stopped short by Justin's quick reach. "Don't run or defend yourselves!" Justin cried.

The soldiers kicked at the backs of their knees, forcing them to the ground, and bound their hands behind them.

Crescens pushed away from his pillar and stepped forward with a cruel, satisfied smile.

"You are just a philosopher like I am," Justin said. "You have no authority to arrest us."

Crescens squatted down to look his opponent in the eye. "I'm not arresting you. Rusticus, the prefect of the city, is arresting you. He got an anonymous tip that you might be a Christian. It looks like you won't be needing this anymore." He tore the philosopher's mantle from Justin's shoulders and laughed. "It was a pleasure to see you again." He turned away.

"Crescens!" Paeon cried from the floor, spitting dust from his lips. Crescens turned back with a sneer.

"You may have Justin's mantle, but you don't have the true philosophy."

In one swift motion, Crescens tore the garment in two and ground it into the pavement underfoot. With a last glance at Justin, he disappeared into the crowd. Jerked to their feet, Justin and his friends were led away by the soldiers.

Only minutes had passed when the cell doors slammed shut. Six figures pulled themselves up from the ground. Justin remained on the floor where he had been shoved.

"I knew this was a bad idea!" Hierax chided. He felt around the dim cell, looking for a way out.

"I'm glad they threw us to the ground," chirped Charito. "It wouldn't feel like a real arrest if I hadn't been thrown to the ground."

Liberianos brushed dried blood from the side of his face. "Any chance they will let us go?"

Euelipistus threw his shoulders back and declared, "I am a servant of the emperor. They can't treat me this way."

"I'm pretty sure the soldiers never got that message!" said Chariton.

Justin threw his hands above his head. "Heavenly Father," he cried out, "since the days of the apostles we have tried to live peaceably in this land. We try to obey all the laws that don't conflict with your Scripture, and we are kind to our neighbors."

Hierax stopped groping along the damp wall and drew near Justin.

"By your grace, we have tried to serve you faithfully and live a life pleasing in your sight. We ask now, Lord, if you are willing, that you would free us from this cell. But if you are not willing, may the fire that takes our lives be the light of your gospel to the world. Amen."

The cell was silent. Then a raspy voice came from a dark corner. "Who is this Heavenly Father? And who are you?"

An old man crawled with obvious pain out of a dark corner of the cell. As he came closer in the dim light, Justin saw that his teeth were scarce, his hair filthy and matted, his hands and feet covered with sores. He smelled worse than he looked.

Justin joined the feeble prisoner on a mound of moldy straw. "My name is Justin. I'm a Christian philosopher."

"I'm Antonius," the man replied. He squinted. "You're not from Rome, are you?"

"No," Justin acknowledged. "I'm a Samaritan, but I was born in Flavia Neapolis, not far from the ruins of Sychem. My grandfather and father were raised as Gentiles."

"And who is this Heavenly Father? A new god?"

"No. He is the Christian God, the only true God."

Antonius was briefly overcome with a fit of coughing that left flecks of spit on his tangled beard. "Why do you call him the only true God? What makes him greater than the other Roman gods?"

"Another man once asked me a similar question," Justin replied. "The famous Jewish Rabbi Trypho."

"So?"

"I told him I was not a Christian from birth. I didn't know anything about the books of Moses or the teachings of Jesus. At first, I sat under a Stoic philosopher, but realized he didn't have any answers. So I experimented with different teachings."

"And I suppose none of them were useful."

"None," admitted Justin. "I found bits of truth in each one, but not one of them ended my search for the truth about life. The great Plato's teachings were helpful, but ultimately deceiving, because they led me to think I had the answers when I really didn't."

"So what does this have to do with the teachings of a Jew known as Christ?"

"One day, when my unsuccessful search for the truth left me discouraged, I ventured into a field near the sea. I often spent time there in contemplation, listening to the waves along the shore and watching the sea breezes bend the crops."

"Did the Heavenly Father appear to you in that field?"

"No, but his messenger did. A pleasant old man was in the field that day. He was so meek and quiet that at first I wasn't aware he was following me. He was looking for a family member who had disappeared in the field. We began to talk, and he told me about God and his son Christ, and showed me his Scriptures."

"Did he find who he was looking for?" Paeon piped up with curiosity. Justin's friends had been quietly listening to the exchange.

"I don't know," said Justin, "but I found the one I was looking for. I found the creator, the father of all things. I found his son,

Jesus Christ, and the salvation that comes only through trusting in him. A flame was kindled in my soul. A love for those who love Christ possessed me. I discovered that the true philosophy is that which comes from the text of the holy Scriptures."

Justin put a hand on the old man's gaunt shoulder. "If you believe in God and look for salvation from his son, you can be freed from your sins, though you are imprisoned in this cell. You may suffer in this dark, lonely place, but you can live a happy life even here."

A muffled rattling of chains echoed in the dark cavern. The scrape of a key in the lock could mean freedom, but Justin knew that this key opened the door to the end. As the soldiers escorted the seven out of the cell, Justin looked back at Antonius. Eyes glittering in the torch light, the old man gave him a slow, silent nod and retreated into the shadows.

Justin and his friends were led before a golden chair flanked on both sides with armed soldiers. Prodded with spears, they were forced to the ground for questioning.

The chair's occupant, with his fist full of roasted meat, took a huge bite and reached for his wine goblet. "I'm Rusticus, prefect of this place," he said, spitting food with each *p*. "The laws of this land command all who dwell here to offer sacrifices to our gods. You are accused of being Christians, atheists who refuse to worship our gods. I give you two choices: obey the gods at once and offer sacrifices, and your lives will be spared. If you refuse, you will be executed."

"Obedience to our Savior Jesus Christ is not worthy of condemnation," Justin replied. "Christianity is the only truth, and I must follow its teachings, even if that disturbs you."

Rusticus snorted. "You are pleased with those teachings?"

"More than pleased. I am convinced."

"What are these teachings that have so convinced you?"

Justin raised himself to his knees. "We worship one God, not many. He is the creator of all that is visible and invisible. The Lord Jesus Christ, the Son of God, who was spoken of by the prophets, teaches the truth and brings salvation. Nothing I say about him can capture his boundless divinity."

"Where do you meet to teach this heresy?"

Justin saw the gleam in the prefect's eye and recognized this obvious ploy to locate other Christians. "We meet wherever we choose," he said. "Our God is not bound by place. He fills the heavens and the earth, and is worshiped and glorified everywhere by his faithful children."

"Enough!" said Rusticus, silencing him with a greasy hand. "Are you a Christian?"

"Yes."

He pointed at Charito. "And you as well?"

"By the grace of God!" she declared.

Turning to Euelipistus, he leaned forward curiously. "Aren't you a servant of Caesar?"

"Yes."

"Are you a Christian as well?"

"I am. Having been freed by Christ and his grace, I have the same hope as the others."

"Then Caesar will appreciate my work today!" He raised a bushy eyebrow at Hierax.

"Yes, I worship the same God," was the response.

"Did Justin make you Christian?"

"I was a Christian when I met Justin, and I will always be one," replied Hierax.

Paeon suddenly broke away from the grip of a guard, jumping to his feet. "I'm a Christian too! I haven't forgotten my promise, Justin!"

The soldier struck him across the face and forced him back to his knees.

"Who taught you about Christianity?" demanded Rusticus.

"My parents taught me."

"I wasn't coerced by Justin either," said Euelipistus. "I willingly came to hear what he had to teach me, but I first learned to be a Christian from my parents."

"And where are they?"

"In Cappadocia, far from here."

In disgust, the prefect turned his sarcasm on Justin. "Do you really believe that if you are scourged and beheaded you will somehow ascend into heaven?"

"I am fully persuaded that I will be resurrected at the end of the world."

"For you, the end of the world is today, unless you sacrifice to the gods."

"No one in his right mind would commit such a sin."

The prefect's face reddened. He lurched to his feet, crumbs flying from his lap. "Unless you obey, you will be punished mercilessly!" he bellowed.

"Our punishment will only give us confidence in our salvation," Justin replied calmly. "There will be a day more fearful than this, when we sit before the judgment seat of our Lord and Savior."

"Do what you will!" yelled Paeon, struggling to his feet again. "We won't sacrifice to idols!"

Rusticus lowered himself into his jeweled chair, nostrils flared, eyes narrowed. "Very well," he growled with controlled anger. "Let those who have refused to yield to the command of the emperor be scourged and beheaded according to our laws!" He drained his wine goblet and signaled to the ranking soldier.

They were dragged out. Limbs bound, clothes torn away, the prisoners were beaten with rods. Between the agonizing blows, they cried out to their God.

"God of heaven and earth, master of all things!" shouted Justin.

"Please accept this sacrifice of obedience. It is an honor to suffer for the sake of Christ."

"Lord!" cried Hierax. "Thank you for your gift of eternal life and the resurrection to come. You are the one true God!"

Unable to move, Justin forced open his eyes and saw a dirty, sandaled foot draw near. Summoning a final scrap of strength, he gazed into the sky and whispered, "I serve no other God." The axe fell swiftly.

When darkness came, a furtive band stole onto the blood-soaked ground and carried away the bodies. Accompanied by quiet weeping, Justin and his friends were laid in a suitable place, to silently await the resurrection.

Justin became known as Justin the Martyr. His writings were later used by Irenaeus, one of the greatest early Bible teachers.

WORSHIP IN THE ANCIENT CHURCH

IF YOU STEPPED back in time to a church service in the early years of Christianity, you would find some very familiar elements and some very different elements. What we know about worship in the ancient church comes from the letters and books of the first Christian writers. The practice of worship varied from place to place, but many of the elements were the same.

MEETING PLACES

Christian worship began in Jewish *synagogues*, because the first Christians were Jews who believed the message of Jesus. The friction between Jews and Christian Jews pushed the early Christians to find their own places of worship. For the first few hundred years, Christianity was illegal in the Roman Empire, so the meetings were usually held in secret. Sometimes they met out in the desert, or in tombs or *catacombs* under the cities. Early Christian fathers said that since God is everywhere at the same time, they could worship anywhere and still be in his presence.

In some cities, all the Christians who lived in that city gathered in one building. In other cities where there were too many, they met by districts. Most of the time, Christians met in private homes, which were remodeled to make room for larger groups. Some of the houses were bigger than others, but most contained an atrium or an open courtyard where the people gathered. Baptismal fonts were installed in these houses, so the presbyters could sprinkle or pour water for baptisms.

When the persecutions ended, these church-homes were torn down and rebuilt to make room for the growing number of worshipers. One of the earliest church buildings, Old St. Peter's Basilica, was 835 feet long, with high ceilings and pillar supports. It became a model for future church construction.

WHAT WORSHIP LOOKED LIKE

No matter where Christians worshiped, the elements of worship remained the same. Justin the Martyr wrote that the church gathered on the first day of the week. During the service, they read the Old and New Testaments, and then the bishop explained the texts they read and encouraged the people to stay true to Christ. The congregation would then stand, in an imitation of the resurrection of Jesus, and pray together.

Prayer was followed by communion, or the Lord's Supper. Bread and wine, slightly diluted with water, were passed out to the church members. (Deacons would take the supper to the sick or elderly who could not attend the service.)

An important source on ancient Christian worship is an early worship manual called the *Didache*, meaning "the teaching." The Didache tells us that during communion, the believers first confessed their sins, and then thanked God for the bread and wine.

The people prayed together again, led by the bishop, and closed by singing, "Amen."

At the end of the service, anyone who was able to give money to the church collection did so, according to their means. The money was used to provide for orphans, widows, and needy travelers.

Baptism was a serious commitment. Hippolytus, a rival bishop of Rome, tells us that Christians had to be instructed in Scripture for three years before they could be baptized. During the instruction period, they were called *catechumens*. The night before a baptism, the catechumen prayed and fasted. He or she would be either naked or dressed in a white robe, and was anointed with oil. The catechumen would climb into the baptismal font, which was usually knee deep, and water would be poured over the head. If the water was deep enough, the person's head was submerged. Often, water was poured three times, to represent the Father, Son, and Holy Spirit. After baptism, the Christian took communion for the first time.

PREACHING

Sermons have been a primary element of Christian worship since the beginning. Most of the writings we have of Augustine or John Chrysostom are their sermons. Next to the Lord's Supper, the sermon was the most important tool for Christian growth. Because of this, Hippolytus reminded his congregation to always be on time for worship. The sermon was open to visitors and usually came first in the service.

An element of worship added by the year 400 was a remembrance of the martyrs. At first it was just a way to honor them, but eventually the congregations dedicated shrines to them. Augustine's mother Monica was known for visiting these shrines until Bishop Ambrose forbade it. The practice of including a martyr's remembrance became a dividing issue in later years.

Ancient Christian worship gave glory to God and promoted unity in the early days of the church. It was a spiritual refreshment for Christians who struggled against the threats of persecution and the temptations of the world.

⊕RIGEN: G⊕D PLANTED IN US THE UNSPEAKABLE L⊕NGING T⊕ KN⊕W

201 AD. ALEXANDRIA, EGYPT.

ORIGEN AWOKE WITH a start, his heart racing. He strained to listen, but heard nothing more than the quiet breathing of his brothers nearby. The voices must have been part of his nightmare. Every night for the last week he had dreamed the same scene.

He is standing in front of the church, sweating, the air so thick and hot that he can hardly breathe. Scattered across the blood-soaked street are the bodies of his Christian friends. Somehow the soldiers have missed him, and he is alone. But instead of escaping, he runs after the soldiers, shouting. He is running as fast as he can, but he is barely moving. His screams come out like whispers. "I'm a Christian too! I want to die for Jesus too! What about me?" One of the soldiers turns and, seeing him, charges toward him in slow motion . . .

"You're focusing too much on the recent persecutions," he told himself, pulling the wool blanket around him again. "Go back to sleep." He closed his eyes and slowly drew in a deep breath.

Crack! The sound of splintering wood brought him to his feet.

He wasn't dreaming this time. He jumped up from his mat on the floor and rushed into the outer room. Soldiers pushed past him, swords drawn.

"Father!" he shouted.

His father's firm voice was muffled as the soldiers surrounded him. "Stay with your brothers, son."

Origen whirled in the doorway and glanced behind him. The six younger boys huddled together in the dark, their eyes wide with fear.

"Leonides, you are under arrest by order of Emperor Severus and charged with treason," proclaimed the centurion, forcing the man to his knees.

Treason. That's what the emperor called it, Origen knew, but it wasn't true. "Christians are not trying to overthrow the government, but the emperor sees us as a threat to his power anyway," he thought. Most of the other church leaders who had been arrested were executed. Origen was afraid of the soldiers, but his father had often told him it was a privilege to die for Christ. When he was a young boy, Origen had promised God he would be willing to die for him.

Behind him, he heard one of his brothers crying. His mother stood pale-faced in the corner. He wanted to comfort them, but he couldn't take his eyes off his father. The soldiers roughly locked Leonides in chains, but he didn't fight back. Origen had never been so proud of his father.

"I'm a Christian!" he shouted, rushing forward. "Arrest me, too!"

"Origen!" His mother rushed to him and clamped her hand over his mouth. "Don't be foolish!"

He wrenched himself free. "Father has taught me so much about the martyrs. If he is going to be arrested, so will I."

"No, Origen, stay with your mother," Leonides called to him

as the soldiers led him through the broken doorway. "Remember what I have taught you." He twisted around to look at his wife.

"Enough!" shouted the centurion. "Say good-bye to your family, Christian." He laughed as they dragged their prisoner outside.

Origen embraced his mother quickly. "I am going with him," he said. "Good-bye, Mother."

"You're not going anywhere!" she cried, grabbing his arm. "You're only seventeen, and I need you."

"It's more important for me to be a witness to Christ!" He pulled away.

"You're not even dressed! Are you going to run out and be a witness in your underwear?"

He looked down at his bare chest and blushed. He had forgotten that he was almost naked, and in front of his mother, too! He ran back into his room and snatched up his tunic and sandals. "I'll catch up with them. They can't have gone far."

But she was blocking the doorway now, with tears pouring down her cheeks. "You heard your father!" she said firmly. "You're not going anywhere, if I have to hide your clothes to keep you here!" She seized the clothing from his hand.

"But, Mother!"

"They're not going to take you both away from me!" she cried. She ran out of the house weeping, the bundle of clothing in her arms.

He kicked the wall in desperation. A little sob behind him made him turn around, and he noticed his brothers still huddled in fear. He crossed the room in three long steps and threw his arms around them. "Everything is going to be fine," he promised. "God will take care of us. Go back to sleep now." He tucked them back into bed and stayed with them until they fell asleep.

The house grew quiet again. He sat up all night, listening for the soldiers and watching the boys toss and turn in their troubled sleep.

"Lord, make my father be a strong witness for you," he prayed. "Comfort my mother, and help her see that I must go too."

But in the morning, when he tiptoed across the remains of the front door to look for his clothes, he saw his mother. Sitting in front of the house in the first rays of dawn, her eyes were calm but her face was stained with tears. "It's only a matter of time now, Origen," she said quietly. "It was God's will, and there is nothing we can do. But it was not his will for you to go too. He has something different for you to do."

When he started to speak, she drew a hand across her eyes and shook her head. "Don't bother looking for your clothes. I buried them."

He looked at her sitting there with her head down and her shoulders slumped. "Mother is willing to die, too," he thought, "but it is harder for her to lose Father." He bent down and kissed the top of her head. "If that's how God wills it to be, then I must accept it. But I'm going to write to Father and encourage him."

It took him only a few minutes to collect the door fragments and haul them to the kitchen, adding them to the wood pile near the fireplace. In his father's room, he found a sheet of papyrus and an inkwell. "Be strong in the Lord, Father," he wrote. "Don't deny Christ because of your concern for us. The Lord will provide for our family."

Several days later, a messenger arrived with the news that Leonides had been beheaded. "I'm sorry," the messenger said, "but I must also tell you that the emperor has seized your husband's property, and soldiers will come to claim this house. You must find somewhere else to live."

"The Lord will protect us," his mother replied bravely. "Origen, help your brothers pack their clothes and books."

One of his mother's wealthy friends invited them to stay with her. "Stay as long as you need to," she said. "I know Origen is training to be a teacher, and he must finish school. Leonides would have wanted that."

He studied hard, thinking of his mother's insistence that God had something important for him to do. "There is a reason why I was born in Alexandria, where we have the biggest library in the world," he thought. He spent many long days at the library, carefully lifting the heavy papyrus scrolls from their shelves and unrolling them on a table to read.

As soon as he earned his teacher's certificate, he got a job teaching literature.

"Just like your father," his mother smiled.

But it wasn't enough money to feed eight mouths. When his classes let out in the evenings, he worked by candlelight for rich neighbors who hired him to copy scrolls by hand.

One evening, he got a visit from a former teacher. Clement was in charge of the church school that taught new believers the catechisms. He was only forty, but his long beard and the concerned wrinkles at the corners of his eyes made him seem older.

"Hello, Origen. How is your mother?"

"She is a brave woman." He offered his friend a chair.

"She has you to encourage her."

"I hear you have ten more catechumens at the church."

"That is true. God keeps blessing the church here! Actually, that's why I'm here." Clement leaned forward in his seat and looked at the young man seriously. "I have good news. I am leaving Alexandria."

Origen wrinkled his forehead. "That's not good news! Where are you going?"

"The emperor doesn't like me any more than he liked your father, so I will oblige him and go away," Clement said. "But it means that Bishop Demetrius needs someone to take over for me at the church school. I told him how smart you are, and how your father gave you such a good education before he sent you to me."

"Thank you, sir."

"I recommended you as my replacement, and he agreed to give you a try."

"I can never replace you, but it is an honor to accept your offer. I will do my best. But I'm sorry to see you go!"

"I'm sorry to leave," Clement said with a sigh. "But I know that God has other plans for me, and I know you will serve the church well."

Clement was right. Origen was a great teacher, and though still a teenager, his students respected him. He and his mother found a small house and kept the boys fed. He began to write books about the Bible and the teachings of the church, and soon was well-known in Alexandria.

"You've been supporting us for several years now, Origen," his mother said one morning. She set a batch of bread dough aside and wiped her hands. "Your brothers are working now, and they make enough money to provide for all of us. Why don't you quit teaching literature and spend all your time teaching at the church?"

"Bishop Demetrius will be happy to have my full attention," he replied with a smile. "I'll have time to teach the Bible to more people this way."

He began to spend all of his time at the church. The emperor's persecution continued, and often Origen visited those who had been arrested and prayed with them before they were executed.

"So many have lost their lives for you, Father," he prayed, "but you have preserved me. If you don't want me to die for you, then I will live for you as best I can."

He decided to get rid of everything that distracted him from his work. He gave away everything but his books and one set of clothing. He taught at the church all day, and stayed up late every night praying and studying Scripture. When he finally let himself sleep, it was on the hard floor. He was afraid too much food or sleep would make him lazy.

"I'm doing so much teaching and writing," he told his mother, "but I still have so much to learn. Father taught me reading and maths and the Bible. But there is much about the world that I don't know." He leaned closer to her, his dark eyes sparkling with excitement. "I'm going to keep teaching, but I'm going to be a student again, too. There is a famous teacher here in the city who can teach me science and philosophy and how the universe works."

"The enemies of Christianity have always called it the religion of uneducated people," she said, smiling. "But an intelligent man like you proves them wrong."

The next day, Origen introduced himself to Ammonius Saccas.

"I have heard of you," the great teacher said. "Why do you want to study philosophy with me? I thought Christians looked down on science."

"When you see the work of an artist, your mind burns to know how and why it was created," Origen replied. "It is the same with the world. God planted in us the unspeakable longing to know the how and why of his great works."

"You're an unusual young man," Ammonius said. "I'd be happy to have you attend my lectures."

With Ammonius, Origen studied the writings of the famous philosopher Plato. At the library, he read as much about philosophy and science as he could, and he kept studying the Bible.

After several years, one of his students at the church school suggested he start his own school of philosophy. "You're such a good teacher, Origen," Heraclas said. "You know Christianity and philosophy, and people need to understand both. If Bishop Demetrius will let me, I can take over for you here at the church. Why don't you start your own school?"

Origen found a wealthy woman who was willing to fund the new school. Soon he had several students who came to study Plato and the Bible with him. They sat on the floor in a circle and took turns answering Origen's questions.

"How do we pursue the best life?" he asked his students.

"We study the truth and learn about ourselves," said one young man.

"We identify evil and flee from it," said another.

"You're both right," Origen replied. "The ancient philosophies teach us many things about truth and lies, about good and evil. We study them because they prepare us to understand Scripture. But when they disagree with what the apostles of the church taught us, we must follow the apostles."

The school continued to grow.

"I'm proud of you," his mother said. "I knew God was sparing you for something special, and you have proved me right. Your father would be proud of you, too."

Origen took her hand and smiled kindly. "Thank you, Mother. I thought you were wrong then, but I understand now that God had something else for me to do."

He kept teaching, and published book after book. The more he studied, the more he needed to write about what he learned. But he couldn't write fast enough to keep up with his brain. So he hired a young man to be his scribe and write while he dictated.

"Please slow down, Sir," the scribe said. "I can't keep up with you." He was scribbling across the page as fast as his fingers could go.

Origen hired another scribe to help the first, and then another. Eventually he had seven scribes working for him so he could dictate several books at a time.

"Tell me about your latest project," Bishop Demetrius asked

one day when he stopped by the church school for an update on the catechism classes.

"It's called a Hexapla," Origen said. "Six versions of the Bible in columns side-by-side so readers can compare them. I'm including my notes to encourage readers to study more."

"A brilliant idea, young man. But don't get ahead of yourself. You still have much to learn."

"I don't think the bishop likes me," Origen told Heraclas later. "He's always reminding me that he knows more than I do."

Heraclas shrugged. "He's been a bishop for many years. He's just trying to give you good advice."

Origen frowned. "I suppose you're right." But he wasn't sure he believed it.

Over the years, Origen became wiser and more popular. The tension between him and the bishop continued to grow.

One winter, Origen took some of his students on a trip to Athens. It was a long journey. On the way, they stopped in the city of Caesarea in Palestine.

"One of the local church leaders has invited us to stay with him," Origen told his companions. "We'll spend a few days here so you can rest from the journey and get to know this great city."

The man who met them at the door was thrilled to see them. "The great teacher Origen in my house!" he exclaimed. "I have read your books. It is truly an honor to share my roof with you and your friends."

"Thank you for your hospitality."

A servant with a water jug bent to wash Origen's feet, dirty from a long day of walking.

"When you are finished here, Philip will bring you some food," the presbyter said. "Then we can talk."

After he had eaten, Origen shared the news from Alexandria with his host as they rested in the garden. "I know you have just arrived," Gaius said, "but I told the other presbyters here that you were coming, and we would be honored if you would spare some time to teach us."

"Your request is a great compliment," Origen said. "But I am a philosophy teacher, not a presbyter. I've never been ordained. I'm not sure it would be right for me to preach to you."

"You have been given a great gift from God. Surely it is right for you to bless us with your gifts."

"I would love to do some teaching while I am here," Origen said thoughtfully. "Let me send word to my bishop and make sure he doesn't object."

Origen sent a messenger back to Alexandria. When the reply came from Bishop Demetrius, it was firm. "Only an ordained presbyter is fit to teach other presbyters. If these men have learning to do, they need to seek training from their bishop."

"His resistance to me is getting frustrating!" Origen thought. "This is not the right answer, but he does have God's authority." He left Caesarea without teaching. But soon Gaius invited him back.

On the second trip, Origen was again asked to teach. "You heard what Bishop Demetrius said. Unless I am ordained, I don't have the authority to teach you."

Gaius shrugged his shoulders. "What's to stop you from being ordained then? Our bishop will ordain you here."

Demetrius can't object to that, he decided. He was ordained without delay, and Bishop Theoctistus of Caesarea invited him to preach to the people. "God has greatly gifted him," Theoctistus told Gaius. "He is as good a preacher as he is a writer. Our people will learn much about the Scriptures from him."

As soon as he returned to Alexandria, Origen was ushered into Demetrius's office. The bishop rose to his feet in anger. "How dare you defy me? You are under my authority, and I specifically ordered you not to preach in Caesarea."

"With all respect, Bishop, you ordered me not to preach while I was not ordained. Now that I am ordained, I saw no reason for you to object."

"You had no right to become ordained without my approval!"

Origen took a deep breath and carefully controlled his voice. "Bishop Theoctistus approved the ordination, and I was in Caesarea, not in Alexandria. You have no authority there."

"This attitude is not appropriate for someone in your position, Origen. The church must discipline you for your actions in Caesarea."

"You must do what you believe is right." Origen turned abruptly and left the room.

"Origen has a brilliant mind," Demetrius thought. "But his brilliance has made him arrogant."

"Demetrius is a godly man," Origen's friends said to each other. "But he is jealous of Origen's talent."

Demetrius called for a meeting of church leaders and argued that Origen was guilty of rebelling against church authority. Most of the other leaders agreed. Origen was stripped of his teaching position at the church and asked to leave Alexandria.

He said good-bye to his mother and left for Caesarea. Theoctistus immediately came to welcome him. "The church in Caesarea disagrees with the council in Alexandria, Origen. Your ordination is valid here. Stay and start a new school."

He already had a list of students anxious to study with Origen. Soon the new school in Caesarea was as popular as the school he had left in Alexandria. He threw himself back into his teaching and writing.

Twenty years passed, and a new emperor came to power.

"Like my body, the empire is not as strong as it once was," Origen said to his students Pamphilus and Antony. "Emperor Decius believes he can restore Rome's power by going back to worshiping the old Roman gods."

"The new law requires all citizens to offer incense to the gods," Pamphilus said. "If we don't have a certificate proving we've offered incense, we'll be arrested."

Pamphilus nodded. "I've heard that some Christians are bribing officials to get false certificates."

"A new emperor, but the same persecution," sighed Origen, shaking his gray head. He thought about the night so many years ago when he saw his father for the last time and his mother hid his clothes. "We must be strong, boys, and confess Christ no matter what the consequences."

A number of Christians in Caesarea were arrested and tortured. Some denied Christ and agreed to sacrifice to the Romans gods. But the others refused and continued to confess Christ. They died in prison.

"These confessors will be honored forever by our Lord and by the church," Origen told his students.

That night he was arrested. At his trial, he refused to offer incense to the Roman gods.

"For such a brilliant scholar, you're a foolish man," declared the Roman proconsul. "For your act of treason, I sentence you to death. But first you will be tortured until you deny your faith in Christ, and the news of your denial will destroy your followers and end this Christ-worship once and for all!"

He lay limp on the filthy floor of his prison cell. The beatings had been severe, and the pain of his broken bones and infected wounds was unbearable. He couldn't think straight enough to pray, so he tried to remember the psalms he had memorized. "Give thanks to the Lord, for he is good," he recited. "His love endures forever."

Every day Pamphilus and Antony gathered the other students to pray for Origen. "He is being starved and tortured in prison," Pamphilus said. "We must pray that God will keep him faithful."

One morning as they were bowed in prayer, a student ran in. "God has answered our prayers!" he cried. "Emperor Decius is dead, and all prison sentences have been overturned. Origen is being released!"

They cheered, and prepared to welcome their teacher home. But Origen was no longer a young man and his body had been broken by the torture. He died on the way home. Christians in the city of Tyre buried him there and sent word to the church in Caesarea.

Pamphilus and Antony wept together.

"This is too great a loss!" Pamphilus declared.

"But we can praise God that our beloved teacher confessed Christ to the end," Antony reminded him. "He is an example to the entire church!"

"He would want us to keep up his work here. What can we do?"

"Well, he had so many good books. We can preserve his library so new students can learn from them," Antony replied. "Why don't you write a book about his life?"

"I am not the writer he was."

"But you knew him better than most of us. Future generations need to know how much he loved his Lord and what he did for the church."

Pamphilus looked at Origen's beloved scrolls, so many of them in his own handwriting. "You're right," he said. "I will tell them." He sat down at the great teacher's desk and began to write.

Origen's brilliant writings inspired generations of Christian thinkers. Pamphilus maintained his teacher's library, and in 307, with the help of his student Eusebius, published his six-volume Apology for Origen while he was in prison. Like his teacher, he died a martyr's death.

CYPRIAN: THIS BODY IS MY SACRIFICE

248 AD. FOOTHILLS SOUTHWEST OF CARTHAGE, NORTH AFRICA.

DURING THE REIGN of Emperor Decius, the empire became very unstable. Worried that the ancient gods had forsaken Rome, Decius commanded all the citizens to demonstrate their loyalty to the gods by offering a public sacrifice...

"Quickly!" A shadowy figure sprinted through the dense bushes. It was a dark night, and only the dim starlight illuminated the hedge of thorns that separated the countryside from the city limits.

Trailing behind the sure-footed guide was an older man dressed in a white linen tunic and a brown cloak. He was escorted by several younger men, their sharp eyes alert to danger. Across their backs bulged packs of food and other supplies, the most carefully wrapped bundles containing scrolls and papyrus for writing.

Urgent whispers ahead of them prodded the small band to move faster. With each step, the underbrush crackled.

"This way," insisted the guide in a low voice, scrambling onto a rock and pointing to an opening in the brush that marked a stony trail leading up into the mountains. "This path will take us far from the city."

A little slower than his younger friends, the man in white hoisted up his garments to keep pace without stumbling. Squinting in the darkness, he winced and plucked at a tree branch tangled in his long, graying beard. As he climbed, the dry twigs beneath his feet gradually gave way to sharp pebbles. He paused and looked over his shoulder toward home.

Stretched across the valley below stood Carthage, her lamps slowly flickering out as the city settled in for the night. Will I ever return? he wondered. He caught a glimpse of moonlight on the Mediterranean Sea beyond the city walls and thought longingly of the deep blue waters. The further away from the sea he climbed, the more the hot air stuck in his lungs.

"The cave I must now call home can never compare to my beloved city," he thought.

A gentle hand settled on his shoulder.

"Come, Bishop Cyprian. We don't have much time."

"Yes, Pontius," he sighed. "I know." But he didn't budge. "What about the others I'm leaving behind? They are facing their deaths and I'm running."

"The church in Carthage needs their bishop," urged Pontius. "You'll be killed for certain if you stay. But if you move to a safe place, you'll still be able to lead your congregation from a distance."

"Yes, yes," Cyprian said sadly. "That is what I keep telling myself." He steadied himself on his assistant's shoulder, and stepped over a boulder.

Following the stars into the mountains, they left Carthage behind.

In the bright light of day, the bustling city was far different from Cyprian's desolate new home.

A soldier stood on a popular street corner in the heart of Carthage. "Under declaration of Emperor Decius, everyone must present themselves for a sacrifice to the gods," he announced, waving a document high in the air. "The gods Saturn and Caelestis will be pleased with your sacrifice."

The magnificent pillars of the pagan temple stood proudly as the citizens beneath them scurried around eager to sacrifice to their gods. In the courtyard, statues of the emperor and the gods were buried knee-high in mounds of flowers and fruit. From there, guards criss-crossed the city looking for those rumored to be Christians.

In a second story window across from the temple, a man stood in the shadows observing the activity below.

"Come away from the window. We don't want to draw attention to ourselves."

Caldonius hastily stepped back from the opening and returned to his chair. "Such a disgrace would never have happened under Emperor Philip," he declared.

"How can such stubbly legs move so fast?" taunted his companion, reclining in the corner. "A goat couldn't move as fast as you do!" Tertullus's pronounced chin and deep dimples blocked out the rest of his features when he smiled.

Folding his arms across his chest, Caldonius shot him an indignant look. "This is no time for—."

A knock at the door interrupted his complaint. They stared at each other in alarm.

"Who do you think it is?" whispered Caldonius.

"Look through the hole and see," Tertullus whispered back. He pointed to a hole the size of his little finger at the top of the door.

Caldonius moved his chair to the door and climbed up, flattening his face against the knot in the wood. He looked at Tertullus in surprise.

"It's Felicissimus," he announced, stepping off the chair and shoving it aside. He waved Felicissimus into the room with a rapid gesture. "What are you doing here?"

Felicissimus crossed the room and faced Tertullus with his hands on his hips. "Where is Cyprian?"

"As I told you some months ago, he is in a safe place," said Tertullus. He didn't get up to welcome his guest.

"Have you seen these?" demanded Felicissimus, flapping a sheet of papyrus in his sweaty hand.

Tertullus sat up and snatched the document away, squinting at the text:

> To the commission chosen for sacrifices at Byrsa: I, Quintilius, son of Demetrius of Carthage, age twenty-four, black hair, dark skin, and scar on my right cheek, have always sacrificed to the gods. Now, in your presence, in accordance with the edict, I have sacrificed and tasted the offerings, together with my wife, two boys, and daughter. I request that you certify this below.

This was followed by a final line in a different hand:

> I, the proconsular, witnessed the sacrifice of Quintilius (and his family) this day.

Tertullus's jowls deflated. He read the certificate a second time. "Quintilius sacrificed to the gods?" he said, shaking his head.

"No," said Felicissimus. "He used his money to bribe a guard to get a false certificate. Christians are giving in to their fears. In Rome, they are sacrificing to the gods to save their lives, and if they are wealthy, they are trying to buy these fraudulent certificates."

Caldonius waddled over to see for himself. "They obviously believe it is better to lie than to sacrifice."

"Neither are acceptable." Felicissimus peered down his nose at Caldonius. "Now where is Cyprian?"

Caldonius squared his shoulders and drew himself to his full height of five-and-a-half feet. "As we said, he is in a safe place."

"In Rome," Felicissimus said, shoving his red face toward Caldonius, "Bishop Fabian was willing to give his life for the church. Yet in Carthage, Cyprian runs like a coward." He pointed out of the window toward the mountains.

"Coward?" Tertullus jumped to his feet. "In case you hadn't heard, the people were rioting and shouting, 'Cyprian to the lions! Cyprian to the lions!' What good would it have done him to stay?"

"If Cyprian isn't willing to be martyred," said Felicissimus, "then he shouldn't be bishop. I was willing to be martyred, and I went through torture." He ripped open the front of his tunic, exposing scars on his neck and chest. "Maybe I should be bishop!"

Caldonius grabbed the document from Tertullus's hand and slapped Felicissimus across the face with it. "You, sir, do not love the unity of the church. We all have experienced torture. We know what it is like to sit in dark cells, deprived of food, smelling the stench of our own sores. We know what it is like to walk down streets where the corpses of the martyrs are displayed for everyone to see. But we love the church and we will follow the one God has ordained."

"Even the church in Rome has questioned Cyprian's judgment."

"Cyprian answered the church in Rome," snapped Caldonius. "He answered all of us in a letter several months ago. His presence only caused problems for the Christians here, but his death would cause even more. From a safe location, he can provide the church government some stability."

"Stability?" repeated Felicissimus sarcastically. "Perhaps he is just afraid to face death!"

Caldonius waved a fist. "Felicissimus, you will control yourself!"

The taller man stepped back.

"Cyprian is our bishop. You are a deacon," Caldonius continued in a more moderate tone. "You will learn your place and serve your church as your bishop requests. In his stead, he has left me and the other presbyters in charge, and you will resist such dissension."

"You, in charge? You send Cyprian a message then, and tell him that he is a coward!"

"I'll deliver the message myself," said Tertullus, walking the deacon briskly out the door. "I'm sure he'll have words for you."

Tertullus kept Cyprian informed of all the news from Carthage. As the persecution continued, the bishop ran the church from a distance, writing letters instructing the presbyters and encouraging those who faced torture. Whenever it was possible, Tertullus or a trusted friend slipped out of town to a secret meeting place where Pontius picked up the letters to Cyprian.

Over the hills and off the stony paths, Pontius carried the messages into a spacious cave. When he returned, Cyprian was often writing at a wooden table given to him by a wealthy friend.

Today, the bishop looked up as Pontius entered. "Hand me the Master," he said.

From a notch in the cave wall, Pontius pulled out a scroll of the writings of Tertullian, a famous theologian from Carthage, and Cyprian's favorite. He set the scroll and a leather sack on the table.

"I bring more letters, Bishop."

Cyprian pushed his inkwell aside and picked up the stack of messages. His face grew sadder as he read them in turn.

"The church of Carthage is a mess," he said, rubbing his tired eyes. "Caldonius and Tertullus were finally set free after being severely tortured for refusing to sacrifice to the gods. But they are the blessed ones. Many have been beheaded." He paused. "I should have been there."

"You did the right thing," Pontius insisted.

The bishop pulled a letter from the pile. "According to this letter, Numidicus's wife . . . you remember Numidicus?"

"Yes, of course," said Pontius. "What about his wife?"

"Numidicus's wife was burned alive as she clung to his side. Half of his body was burned with hers, but he didn't die. So the onlookers stoned him until he passed out. They thought he was dead and left his body, but his daughter crept in and dragged him out."

"Will he survive?"

"Caldonius seems to think so. Many have come to faith through his obedience." He touched the scroll on the table. "The Master Tertullian was right when he said that 'the blood of the martyrs is the seed of the church.' I am going to suggest that we promote Numidicus to presbyter."

Pontius took a seat next to the bishop. "What about Felicissimus?"

"Caldonius says that Felicissimus honorably endured the torture as well. But now he is telling everyone that I am a coward and not the rightful bishop of Carthage. He set himself up as bishop in the district of Byrsa, rejecting the church's authority."

"Not the rightful bishop? How can he say that? Haven't you been running the church from here for months? Haven't you sent encouraging letters to those who fear martyrdom? How dare he?"

"He and several others have been saying this for years," sighed Cyprian. "When I became bishop I had only been a Christian for two years. Felicissimus and others seemed to believe that Donatus was wrong when he called me to succeed him as bishop. That, and now my running during persecution, has only made them hate me more."

"Dividing the church of Christ is not right."

The bishop nodded. "Felicissimus has gone too far," he agreed.

"What are you going to do?"

"I'm not sure yet. I have other important issues to deal with at the moment." Cyprian picked up his quill again. "Those who have gone through the persecution and survived are calling themselves the Confessors. They are taking it upon themselves to re-admit to fellowship the lapsed, who forsook Christ at the altar of the gods to save their lives, but now want to come back to the church. Caldonius wants to know what he should do."

Pontius stoked the fire in the cave, stirring up a wisp of smoke with his stick. "Shouldn't we forgive them even after their desertion?"

Cyprian smiled at his gracious friend. "Forgive, absolutely, but only when they have proven they are repentant."

"How do we know they are repentant?"

"It is too easy for them to deny Christ, sacrifice to a false god, and then return to the church as if nothing happened. We need to call a church council to decide the matter for good, and I need to return to my church. We must pray that God will make it so." He bent over a fresh stack of papyrus and began to scribble.

As the months passed, the persecution slackened. Cyprian insisted on abandoning his cave and returning to Carthage. The slow clop-clop of his donkey's steps and Pontius's cautious voice alerted Caldonius, who was waiting for them in front of his house.

"Welcome back!" Caldonius threw his arms around Cyprius, kissing his cheek. "The church will rejoice to have her bishop back."

"It is good to be in Carthage again and to see you well, after all you have been through," said Cyprian, gripping his friend's shoulder. "We have a lot of work to do."

"I sent invitations to all the African bishops as you requested," Caldonius said. "They will be here for the council in a matter of days."

"Good."

Pontius unloaded the donkey and followed them into the house.

A few days later, the tiled courtyard echoed with chatter as the bishops greeted one another. Their bright robes fluttered like colorful birds among the pillars and potted plants. Many of them, replacements of those who had lost their lives in the persecution, were young, and introduced themselves eagerly. In the center of the activity, on a low couch, sat Cyprian. As bishop of the host city, he would lead the council.

"Friends," he called out, rising. "We have a lot to discuss."

The courtyard fell quiet as the bishops settled into their seats. Cyprian opened the meeting with prayer and sat down.

"It is good to see so many bishops in one place." He smiled. "A united church is a church in the bonds of love. It is a church that reflects the unity between Christ and the Father. Christ commanded us to be at peace. When we meet like this and agree as a council of bishops, we maintain that peace."

Heads nodded in agreement.

"First," he said, "we must address the recent actions of Felicissimus."

The council fidgeted.

"His disruptive attitude dishonors Christ and cannot be allowed to continue. The church of Carthage has officially excommunicated him for his actions."

"You cannot do that!" burst out one of the bishops.

"We can, and we must," replied Cyprian calmly, waving the man back to his seat. "Felicissimus has challenged the validity of this office and continues to reject the authority of our presbyters. A man cannot have God as his father if he will not have the church as his mother!"

The bishops eyed one another, but no one challenged him.

"However," Cyprian continued, "he is rightly concerned about the lapsed. I am too. But I do not believe we should allow people who have not repented to return to the church."

He stood and began to pace as he spoke. "We look with favor on the Confessors, for they have a good name and we do not doubt their virtue. We cling to them with eagerness. They refused to wear the crown of the devil, so now the crown of the Lord waits for them in heaven. You Confessors have returned from your battle, and your mother church welcomes you into her arms. Let no one speak ill of the sacrifice these brothers and sisters have made."

When he paused, an old bishop rose respectfully. "Well spoken, Bishop Cyprian. We all agree that the Confessors hold a special position in our church, but what about the lapsed?"

Cyprian's smile faded as he shook his head. "For these, what misery! Many of them did not even wait to be apprehended by the soldiers. They ran eagerly to sacrifice. They fled from physical death and embraced eternal death by denying the name of Christ. They feared the loss of family, wealth, land, and body. They didn't even try to withstand the torture! Now they want to come back?"

"Should we not forgive them, as the Confessors wish?" asked the old bishop.

"The Confessors have kind hearts," replied Cyprian. "But our Lord demanded that we be willing to forsake father, son, mother, and daughter for the sake of the gospel. Jesus told the rich young ruler he couldn't become a disciple unless he was willing to give up everything he had. If anyone rashly believes he can forgive sins or improve the Lord's commands, he does not help the lapsed. Instead he only hurts them. Jesus taught that whoever confesses him before men, he will also confess before the Father, but whoever denies him, he will also deny."

He turned to the council with downcast eyes. "If the lapsed do not repent and prove their sincerity, they should not be welcomed back into the church."

"Those are strong words from a bishop who ran from confessing Christ!" cried a red-faced man, pointing a long finger at Cyprian.

Cyprian shut his eyes and drew in a deep breath. "I will bear the label of coward forever," he thought. Aloud, he said, "They may be strong words, but they come from Scripture, not this bishop!"

The angry man returned to his seat, glaring.

The council found it difficult to agree on what to do with the lapsed. They met many times before they finally decided to examine each case separately. Those who bought false certificates of sacrifice were allowed to return after they repented and received the approval of their local bishop. Those who sacrificed would be restored only on their deathbeds. Those who refused to admit guilt would never be restored to the church.

For the next few years, the empire knew peace again. Cyprian returned to his church, but Felicissimus and his followers continued to taunt him about fleeing to the mountains. Despite his attempts to explain himself, and Pontius's impassioned defense, the accusations continued—until Cyprian was given another chance to prove himself.

When the cruel Valerian became emperor, Christians were once again the target of persecution. In Carthage, Bishop Cyprian was singled out. Soldiers escorted him to the private offices of Aspasius Paternus, the proconsul of Africa. Paternus stood face-to-face with the bishop he had heard so much about, peering at him in silence.

He sat down at his desk and adjusted his fine Roman garment. "Are you Cyprian?"

"I am Cyprian, a Christian and a bishop."

"What does that mean?"

Cyprian took a slow, deep breath and tried to slow his racing heart. "It means that I recognize no gods other than the one true God. He made heaven and earth, the sea and everything that is in them. I serve this God and pray to him day and night, for myself, for all men, and for the safety of the emperor."

The proconsul raised an eyebrow. "You are, therefore, unwilling to change your mind?"

"A good mind knows God and cannot be changed."

"Then you are willing to leave your home and be exiled in the city of Curubis, according to the law of Emperor Valerian?"

Cyprian swallowed and tried to appear unbothered by the sentence. "I will be exiled before I deny my God," he declared.

Paternus turned away as if they were finished. The guards took Cyprian by the elbows and began to usher him out of the office.

"Wait!"

The guards halted, turning Cyprian to face the proconsul again.

"Who are the presbyters in this city?" Paternus demanded.

"It is not for me to reveal who they are."

"I will find them myself!" Paternus exclaimed with clenched fist. "Take him away!" He dismissed the bishop with a wave of the hand.

Cyprian packed what he was allowed to take and rode, with Pontius, to Curubis. The city wasn't far from Carthage. The climate was endurable, and he was well-known there. People came from the outlying areas to visit him and bring him gifts.

"Praise God for sending you to us," they said. "Some of the other bishops have been sentenced to hard labor in the salt mines."

Cyprian sent Pontius to deliver money and care packages to the bishops in the mines. "Perhaps our gifts will help offset their pain."

But Pontius soon returned with a grave report. "Valerian has issued a new declaration ordering an intensified persecution," he said. "Bishops are no longer to be banished. They are to be executed."

The new proconsul, a big man named Galerius, ordered Cyprian back to Carthage. There he lived under house arrest, waiting for his trial, for a full year.

He was reading in his small garden one day when Pontius dashed in with urgent news. "Cyprian! Galerius is coming for you again. They say it is for the last time." He bent over with his hands on his knees, trying to catch his breath.

"How long do I have?" asked Cyprian, looking up from his book. He was reading his beloved Tertullian.

"Galerius is in Utica, twenty-five miles from here," answered Pontius. "It won't be long until the soldiers arrive to take you to him."

"I do not want to die in a city other than Carthage," said Cyprian calmly. "How will my death encourage the church here if it happens in another town?"

"I have an idea. You have friends here who have offered to help you escape, but you have refused."

"Yes, and I still refuse." The bishop rose regally from his bench.

"You do not have to flee the city," Pontius continued, "but you could hide in the city, and make Galerius come to you."

"And then I can die here instead of Utica." He nodded. "Yes, that is what I will do. But when he arrives in Carthage, I will turn myself in."

He drew the Tertullian volume to his chest and held it tenderly. "What an honor it must be to shut one's eyes for only a second in this world, and then to open them in the next, and see Christ."

When the proconsul's soldiers arrived at Cyprian's house, he was already gone. His neighbors suggested that he had fled persecution once again. But when Galerius reached Carthage several hours after his advance regiment, Cyprian turned himself in as he had promised.

Two officers were sent to accompany him to the Praetorium. A curious crowd followed. The trek was long and rigorous in the hot

African sun. Cyprian's tunic was soon drenched in sweat.

"Sir, would you like a change of clothes?" asked one of the officers.

Cyprian smiled. "Why should I make myself comfortable for death?"

Escorted further, Cyprian was brought before Galerius in the Praetorium. The crowd was forced to wait outside, but his closest friends were allowed to accompany him.

Galerius towered above Cyprian. Behind him, the council members sat quietly.

"So you are the reason I had to interrupt my business!"

Cyprian was silent, his eyes unblinking. Galerius turned his back to him and faced the court. "You are Thascius Cyprianus?"

The bishop cleared his throat and replied to the back of the proconsul's head. "I am."

"You call yourself a leader of these sacrilegious people?"

"I do."

Galerius swung around and returned Cyprian's defiant stare. "Our holy emperor commands you to sacrifice!"

"This body is my sacrifice for Christ the king."

Galerius held the bishop's unwavering gaze for a moment, then broke off and turned back to the members of the court. They spoke to one another in low voices. Cyprian couldn't make out the conversation, but he showed no interest, continuing to look straight ahead.

It took the court little time to write out their judgment. Galerius stepped forward again and read from a clay tablet. "You have lived sacrilegiously and have encouraged others to join you in your criminal activity. You have set yourself up as an enemy of the Roman gods and their religious laws. The holy emperor has failed to change your mind about worshiping him despite your exile. Therefore, since you are the instigator of serious crimes, you will be an example to those who have joined your wickedness." His thick lips curled into a bitter smile as he drew a sausage-like finger across his throat. "For these crimes, Thascius Cyprianus shall be beheaded."

Cyprian had waited for this day for years. At last he could prove his dedication to Christ! He had planned to give a speech, but when he opened his mouth, all he could say was, "Thank you, Lord."

He was ushered out. At the back of the room, he passed his friends, who stood in silence with tear-streaked faces. Pontius reached for his arm and said, "I want to be beheaded with you."

Cyprian smiled gratefully as he was dragged away. News of the judgment had spread to the courtyard, and the crowd outside was agitated. Angry and curious, they followed the condemned man and his escorts to the hillside gardens of Sexti. They stopped in a green clearing.

"May I have a moment?" Cyprian asked the guard who had offered him a change of clothes.

The soldier glanced at his centurion, who nodded. "Make it fast."

He took off his cloak and knelt silently in prayer. After a few moments he got back on his feet and took off his tunic, handing it to Pontius.

"Bring out the executioner."

A tall, muscular soldier stepped forward with a heavy sword and guided Cyprian, clad only in his linen undergarments, to his last seat as bishop.

Cyprian turned to the crowd of supporters. "Please show some kindness to this man and pay him for his services," he cried.

The assembly murmured, but several hands came forward. Pontius collected the money and gave the executioner twenty-five gold pieces. Then he embraced the bishop and tied a bandage over Cyprian's eyes.

The executioner guided his victim into position. Someone at the front of the crowd boldly tossed his cloak under the bishop's head. The blood-soaked relic of a martyr would bring a good price later.

The experienced hands that held the sword began to tremble. Never had the executioner seen such resoluteness in a condemned man, or such generosity in the witnesses. He aligned his sword with the outstretched neck before him, but he couldn't swing. Instead he nudged the blade into the dirt and drew back to steady himself.

"Executioner!" shouted the centurion. "You will follow through."

"Yes sir," was the reply. But he didn't move.

"This is ridiculous!" The centurion marched over and yanked the sword from the ground, with a menacing glare at the executioner. "I will do it myself. It is an honor to serve the emperor."

"It is an honor to serve the king," Cyprian whispered.

With a single decisive swing, the bishop's head fell from his body, preaching his last sermon.

After Cyprian's martyrdom in 258, Emperor Valerian became a prisoner of the Persians, who attacked the empire and captured 37 cities. Christianity remained an illegal religion, but the persecutions ended for a while, and the church enjoyed forty years of peace without harassment from the government.

Constantine: With this you will conquer

312 AD. NORTHERN ITALY.

SUFFERING UNDER THE severe persecution of Emperor Diocletian, Christians prayed for deliverance. When the emperor retired to become a cabbage farmer, he installed several men to run the empire in his place. But each wanted it for himself. In the west, the battle for ultimate power was fought between Constantine the Great and Maxentius. With Maxentius holed up in Rome, Constantine began his march through Italy...

The brilliant sun passed to the other side of the earth, casting a golden shadow across the hill overlooking the city of Segusio. Riding from the west, between the sun and the city gates, was a bold figure. His royal armor, draped with a red mantle, glowed against the sun. Urging his horse across the hillside to meet his troops, he looked as strong as marble, with a pillar for a neck and a jaw of brass.

"Con-stan-tine! Con-stan-tine!" chanted a chorus of soldiers.

He gazed at the city that refused to fall. The town garrison had defended it for several days. Finally the walls gave way to the pounding of catapults and rams, but still the garrison commander refused to surrender. "Collect whatever wood you can find and pile it up against the gates," Constantine commanded. "Then light it."

The soldiers spent the night cutting down trees and dragging them to the walls. By early morning, black smoke drifted over the city as the gates burnt to the ground.

Constantine galloped to the front lines and addressed his soldiers. "Do not pillage. Do not harm the townspeople. Remember that this is a war of liberation. Defeat to tyrant Maxentius! In the name of the Unconquered Sun, to victory!"

"To victory!" A massive shout roared over the hillside as the army poured through the smoking gap in the city's defenses. The clash of swords filled the air, but in a matter of minutes, it was over. The garrison surrendered. Constantine rode into the city to see flames sweeping through houses near the gates.

"Exchange your swords for buckets!" He leaped off his horse and grabbed a water jar from a deserted market stall. "Find a well. We can't let this city burn to the ground!"

The townspeople helped the army put out the fires and restore order to the city. A few men dressed as local peasants approached Constantine, and he drew them into a doorway.

"Didn't we tell you it could be taken, my lord?" said one with a smug grin.

"You are the best spies in the empire."

"Your satisfaction is our reward."

"Right, plus the gold I paid you," said Constantine with a wry smile. "Now I have another job for you and your men, Gallio."

"Anything you wish," replied Gallio, nodding.

"Make your way to Turin. Blend in there as you did here, but spread the word that this is a war of liberation. Tell them what happened here and assure them that if they surrender peacefully, their city will not be destroyed."

"As you wish, my lord." With quick bows, the men set off.

Word spread that Constantine was on the move. Miles away, in Rome, Maxentius paced before the prefect of his Praetorian Guard, who had joined him in his palace chambers. "Are my soldiers blind? Or is there a better reason why I was taken by surprise?"

Prefect Volusianus had a soothing voice when he was trying to calm the emperor. "We moved the army from Segusio to Raetia based on strong reports. We didn't know that those reports were rumors started by Constantine himself."

"He is good at starting rumors. He has everyone believing that I am a tyrant!" Maxentius swung at a vase on the table beside him and frowned as it shattered across the floor tiles.

"He will not move any further," assured Volusianus. "A messenger has been dispatched to General Pompeianus at Verona. The heavy cavalry are headed to Turin to intercept Constantine's army."

"Good."

"Will you ride out to meet the enemy?"

The emperor turned and walked toward his balcony. "There is no need," he said over his shoulder. "He can be no match for the heavy cavalry, and Pompeianus is a skilled soldier." He leaned over the railing. "Do you see this city?"

"She's beautiful."

"She has withstood her enemies for centuries," said Maxentius, more confident now as he looked out over the strong fortifications. "I don't think Constantine will manage to take her now."

Emperor Constantine and his army marched on Turin. The remaining soldiers from Segusio's garrison had joined his forces. The emperor rode next to Gaius, his trusted general and friend.

"Do we have a good description of this heavy cavalry?"

Gaius wiped sweat from his high forehead. "Yes, sir. They are well-trained horsemen. The soldiers and horses are fully protected by tunics of armor. Their long spears keep them well out of the reach of attackers. They're slow moving, but they can break the front lines of any army."

"What is your plan?"

"Moving to Turin takes us further east. We could take the passages through the Apennines mountains to the south."

"No, if we do that, we leave our flank unprotected from Pompeianus in the north. He's too dangerous. We will continue to Turin."

"And when we arrive?"

"When we arrive, you'll dazzle me with a brilliant strategy!" Constantine slapped his commander on the back and rode off.

Turin was a great city and well worth the expense to protect. When Constantine's army arrived, the heavy cavalry they had heard so much about were spread across the fields in front of the city.

Gaius galloped up to Constantine. "We are ready, sir."

"The men have been instructed?"

"Yes, sir."

Constantine turned his horse to face his army. "In the name of the Unconquered Sun, to victory!"

The soldiers raised their swords high and cheered. "To victory!"

Gaius led the charge, the army following in formation. The air was heavy with the scent of earth and horse manure, as the pounding hooves kicked up clods of soil. Behind the foot soldiers, catapults rumbled across the rocky ground.

The two armies braced for a collision. But as Maxentius's metal-clad cavalry prepared to break through the first line of attackers, Constantine's army split. Half of them passed to the left, and the other half to the right, leaving the armored horses blazing through the empty space in the middle.

Stunned, and realizing that something was wrong, the cavalry slowed, attempting to turn their horses around. Constantine's foot soldiers quickly surrounded them. But instead of attacking the armed riders, they struck at the horses' unprotected legs, slashing the big tendons with their swords. The horses collapsed, toppling over on their riders. Constantine's army threw themselves at the horsemen trapped in their heavy armor.

In the thundering chaos, a few of the cavalry managed to reach the Turin gates, but the residents had barricaded themselves inside. The horsemen turned and fled away from the city, disappearing in a cloud of dust.

Gaius rode up to Constantine, his helmet missing. "The enemy is retreating, my lord!"

"Good. Let them. We need to regroup for the night. Tomorrow we will take the city."

In the morning, Constantine's army rose to the surprise of a warm welcome. The gates were flung open and city officials came out to greet the conqueror. Stories planted by Constantine's spies and the defeat of Maxentius's special forces assured them that they were better off to surrender. Men from the city joined Constantine's army, ready to fight against Maxentius.

Constantine's spies had already moved on to Milan and spread the news that he was there to liberate the people. When the army arrived, the city offered no resistance. Like Turin, the people of Milan welcomed the army, allowing Constantine to give his men a brief rest before they marched on Maxentius's greatest northern defense, Verona.

In Verona, General Pompeianus called his officers to a council of war. Their nervous conversation echoed through the great hall as the general entered.

"We need more time," said one commander.

"No, we're ready now," another insisted.

A third raised his voice. "He beat the heavy cavalry! How can we be sure we're ready?"

"We do need more time," said Pompeianus, dropping his helmet on the table and taking a seat. "We'll buy some at Brixia."

The officers leaned forward to hear his plan.

"Brixia stands between here and Verona. Since it has few defenses, Constantine will expect it to surrender like Milan. We'll surprise him by sending our heavy cavalry and our standard cavalry to stall his army."

"But what about here?" asked a commander. "If we send troops to Brixia, there are fewer here to defend Verona."

"I have already sent messengers to Rome requesting more soldiers. Prepare for battle." The general tucked his helmet under his arm and strode out of the room.

During the next few weeks, Rome geared up for a celebration. Maxentius had announced a festival in honor of his fifth year as emperor. Rumor had it he was trying to distract his subjects from the war.

Dashing through the hallways of the palace, Volusianus charged unannounced into the emperor's chambers. "Brixia is taken!"

Maxentius, huddled with city officials over written plans for his celebration, turned slowly to Volusianus.

"Prefect, it is good of you to join us. I was just telling our friends here how we have nothing to fear from Constantine. Our celebration will go on as planned."

Volusianus bent his head. "Yes, sir. Forgive the interruption, sir."

The emperor rose from the table. "Gentleman, please excuse the prefect and I for a moment."

The room emptied immediately. Maxentius turned an angry scowl to the commander of his personal guard.

"Brixia may have fallen, but Constantine has to get past Verona to get to Rome," he insisted. "Verona is a heavily guarded city. He hasn't met our great defenses there."

"He is doing so now. He pushed our heavy cavalry all the way back there. General Pompeianus is requesting reinforcements."

"Our forces will stay in Rome." Maxentius walked across the room to call the planners back. "No matter what happens elsewhere, the usurper will never be able to break through these walls."

"Then, my lord, might I ask…" He paused.

"Yes?"

"If the walls of Rome will hold, what's the harm in sending our troops to Verona?"

Maxentius swept out of the room without answering. "I know that look," the prefect said to himself. "I'd better have a back-up plan, just in case."

Thousands of fiery arrows crossed the sky of Verona like shooting stars.

"Charge!" Gaius bellowed. The second wave of soldiers advanced with their shields locked tightly together, repelling incoming arrows.

Nearby, Constantine conferred with his other commanders. Several scouts had returned with a report.

"The walls against the Adige River are weak. There is a shallow crossing on the east where catapults can get through."

Constantine looked over the city. The front walls still held and the siege was already several days old. He watched his men trying to scale the walls, but they were being driven back or killed before they reached the top.

"Keep the catapults focused here," he ordered. "But send three across the river and take them to the south walls. Perhaps we can break through where they are weaker."

Inside Verona, the pounding catapults deafened the city.

Pompeianus stood just inside the gates arguing with one of his officers.

"With respect, General, this is madness!" cried the officer. "If you leave the city, you will be killed."

"We have forces available in Venetia and Istria," the general insisted. "If I can get out of the city, I can bring them here." Another volley from the catapults shook the gates. "I'm sure the emperor has his reasons for not sending reinforcements, but we need them—now!"

"How will you make it out of the city?"

"I have a plan. Defend these gates until I return!"

When darkness fell, Pompeianus set his plumed helmet aside and dressed as a peasant. He crept out of the city, following the river downstream.

A week later, Constantine's soldiers were still hammering Verona when a scout delivered the message that another army was marching on their position.

"Pompeianus?" asked a bewildered Constantine. "He should be in the city feeling the brunt of our attack! When did he escape?"

"I don't know, my lord," said the scout, "but I got close enough to see the commander's face, and I'm certain it is Pompeianus."

"How long until they get here?"

"A matter of hours."

"If we lose this battle, we lose it all," said Constantine, turning to an officer. "Regroup."

The army pulled back from the walls and fell into ranks. They waited until the enemy had come so close they could hear the orders Pompeianus was shouting to his officers. Constantine turned his horse to face his men, thrusting his sword into the air with a powerful arm. "They have resisted us until now. Defeat is not an option. In the name of the Unconquered Sun, to victory!"

"To victory!"

In front of the city walls, the two armies collided. Constantine fought like a tornado, swift and furious, twisting to meet his enemies on all sides. One by one, he picked off his attackers, his soldiers fighting courageously beside him.

The siege of Verona that had lasted for days ended with those few hours of battle. When Pompeianus was found dead on the field, his men fled. Constantine's army collected weapons from the fallen bodies and rounded up the wandering horses.

Exhausted, hungry, and bleeding, Constantine withdrew to his tent. He sat on the edge of a bearskin-covered cot and dismissed the servant who followed him in with a basin of water. He had lost hundreds of men, and it would now take him longer to reach Rome.

"Can I really take Rome if I barely took Verona?" he wondered.

Gaius poked his head through the canvas flap covering the entrance. "Sir, I have word. Verona will surrender."

"Good."

Gaius drew up a wooden stool. "Sir, the officers, myself included, are concerned that you put yourself in harm's way today." He pointed to his friend's bleeding arm. "You are the emperor. Is it not our duty to do the killing for you?"

"How can I convince my men of the virtue of victory if I am not willing to risk my life?" He absently examined the gash in his arm. "I can't tell which blood is mine and which is that of my enemies."

"We've lost significant numbers."

"I'm aware. Any captured enemy soldiers willing to join my army may do so without penalty."

He dipped a towel in the water basin and pressed it against his wound.

"Yes, sir. They will be treated fairly." Gaius stood. "The hardest part is yet to come, sir, but you are the victor today."

"Maxentius will seek the help of the Roman gods," said

Constantine. "I will seek the blessing of my god, the Unconquered Sun."

"We will need the help of all the gods to take Rome."

"Then pray to all of them, Gaius, even my mother's Christian god. I'm sure she is doing so even now."

It was October, six months after Constantine began his march to Rome. Maxentius ignored his enemy's advance and continued with his plans to celebrate his anniversary as ruler. An expensive spectacle might convince the people they had nothing to fear from the usurper.

The festival began with a parade of the emperor's Praetorian Guard. Spears in hand, decked in gleaming gold armor and scarlet cloaks, they marched as one body through the Via Sacra, the heart of the city. As they passed by, the people cheered proudly, falling into step behind them.

The parade ended at the Circus Maximus, the open-air stadium built for horse-drawn chariot races. The people jostled to get into the Circus and find a place where they could see. Chariot teams, identified by the colors they wore, waited at one end of the oval tracks, ready for the emperor's word.

Maxentius appeared at his podium with a benevolent smile and signaled for the races to begin. He took his seat next to Volusianus.

As the fans screamed for their favorite teams, the chariots flew around the track. They rammed each other, trying to knock off the other riders, and crashed in tangled heaps of splintered wood and flailing horses.

When the dust of the first race settled, Maxentius stood to announce the winner. In the hush came a clear shout from the stands: "Maxentius is afraid of Constantine! Constantine is undefeatable!"

Hidden in the crowd was Constantine's rumor mill, Gallio.

His shout gave way to thousands as the excited crowd picked up the chant. Maxentius demanded silence, but he couldn't shut down the uproar. Volusianus and his guards rushed the stunned emperor out of the Circus.

"I must consult the Sibylline Books for a prophecy," said Maxentius in a panic. The Sibylline Books contained prophecies written as poetry, and Maxentius knew his ancestors had consulted them often. Now he hoped they had an answer for him. "I must know the outcome of this battle. Send for the priest."

"We cannot let Constantine march on Rome," Volusianus demanded. "Segusio, Turin, Milan, Brixia, Verona, all have either fallen to him or surrendered."

The emperor turned to him with a face distorted by anger. "I am aware of my army's failure!"

"We have let Constantine walk to a mere few miles from Rome," Volusianus continued boldly. "He will be here in another day or two."

"I am in control, Prefect. I will decide how to handle this when I have received the oracle."

An ornately-dressed priest arrived in the emperor's chambers. "I bring the Sybilline prophecy you requested, my lord," he declared with a grand bow.

"Well?"

"The enemy of Rome will perish, my lord!"

It was the assurance Maxentius needed. He dismissed Volusianus with orders to prepare hastily to meet Constantine on the battlefield. The favorable prophecy spread throughout the city, and the troops swaggered with confidence to their barracks.

That night, Constantine's troops set up camp just north of Rome. They would cross the river in the morning and storm the city gates. Constantine ordered them to rest before this final battle, and turned in early himself. But his sleep was troubled, and his bed grew damp with sweat. Images of fallen soldiers cluttered his dreams. Suddenly, he sat up. Bursting from his tent in only his undergarments, swinging a lantern, he rushed to wake Gaius. The guards on duty reacted with alarm, but he brushed past them and ran into the general's tent.

"Gaius! Get up!"

Even in his sleep, Gaius kept a hand on his sword. Startled by Constantine's call, he leaped out of his cot, swinging the blade just short of the emperor's neck. "Sir?!" He dropped back as his eyes adjusted to the darkness. "Sir, what's wrong? I almost killed you!"

With a sweep of his arm, Constantine cleared a table in the middle of the tent and threw a piece of parchment on top. "Gaius, I've had a dream, a vision. This symbol——." He pointed excitedly to the parchment. "We must put this symbol on the shields of our soldiers."

Gaius reached for the lantern and leaned over the parchment. In Constantine's strong hand were written two Greek letters, one on top of the other.

"The Christian symbol?" asked Gaius, puzzled.

"Yes, the first two letters of the name of Christ."

"The Christian god? Sir, I don't understand. Why are you so excited about this?"

Constantine leaned over the table, his chiseled features even sharper in the lantern light. "It is the symbol of my mother's religion. I prayed to all of the gods, and then I had a dream. This sign appeared in the sky with the words 'with this you will conquer' written above it."

"The Christian god has chosen to favor you," agreed Gaius. He sheathed his sword and threw a cloak around his shoulders. "Such a sign shouldn't be ignored. I will order all the troops to draw this on their shields." He hurried out of the tent.

The pink dawn was rising over the seven hills of Rome as Maxentius moved his army out of the city and along the Tiber river toward the narrow Milvian Bridge. Pontoons were erected across the river north of the bridge to allow the soldiers to cross more quickly.

Maxentius had to admit that Volusanius had devised a clever strategy in a short time. The prefect would lead his Praetorian Guard across the bridge and attack Constantine's camp by surprise. They would kill as many as they could before the enemy even realized they were under attack. Maxentius would lead another force across the river further downstream, and march north to reinforce the prefect's troops a few hours later. Volusianus would then signal his army to move back across the river, hoping the enemy would chase them across the pontoons. When his forces were safely on the other side, the pontoons would be loosed, and the enemy would be stranded mid-river, an easy target for the archers on the city walls. "It will work," Maxentius told himself. "The enemy of Rome will perish, that's what the prophecy said."

Volusianus and his Guard snuck along the river to unleash their surprise. Swords brandished, they pounced on Constantine's camp, slaughtering hundreds of soldiers still half asleep.

But the camp was soon fully awake and it took only moments for Constantine's men to grab their swords and join the fight. Battle horns sounded. "Charge!" ordered Constantine. "Raise your shields to God!" Thousands of shields bearing the Christian symbol were lifted high as they mounted a swift defense.

Constantine's forces fought bravely, driving Volusianus back. The prefect suddenly realized that the enemy had spread out, trapping his soldiers along the river. Volleys of arrows rained down on his dwindling forces. They were not going to have the head start across the river that he had expected. He watched anxiously for Maxentius and his reinforcements to arrive.

It was late morning before they appeared. Maxentius was confident in the prophecy, and he was sure that Volusianus had already defeated the enemy by now. But as he drew near, he saw that Constantine had pushed the prefect's army right to the riverbanks, and many of his soldiers were forced to jump into the river or be run through with a sword. The bodies of many already littered the banks, drowned by their heavy armor. "No, no," he thought, "this is not supposed to happen!"

He wheeled his horse around and shouted to his generals. "Retreat! Retreat! We'll fight from the city walls!"

They fled back toward the bridge. It wasn't wide enough for the hundreds of soldiers rushing to get across. Maxentius was trapped behind them. He turned in the saddle and saw the enemy closing in behind him.

Constantine drove his troops toward the bridge, swinging his sword. He looked up and met Maxentius's fearful eyes, and in that moment, he knew he had won. He jutted out his powerful chin and hoisted his sword.

"Charge the bridge!" yelled Constantine. "Defeat to the enemy of Rome!"

The enemy of Rome! Desperately, Maxentius urged his horse across the bridge, leaping over the bodies of fallen soldiers. The air was heavy with smoke as fiery arrows criss-crossed the river. He knew Constantine was on his heels. "Just a little further and I'll be through the gates."

Constantine raced toward the bridge. His soldiers were driving what was left of the enemy onto the bridge and the pontoons. Panicking, Maxentius's forces shoved each other into the river as they tried to get across to the city.

Maxentius pushed his horse over the crowded bridge, trampling those who stood in his way. The stone pavement was slippery with blood. Almost there. An arrow zinged past his head and struck his horse between the ears. The beast stumbled, and as he went down on his knees, he tossed his rider over his head.

Maxentius hit the water with a smack that took his breath away. The heavy armor pulled him to the river bottom, and he clawed at it frantically. But the water began to fill his lungs, and as he stopped struggling, the current dragged him downstream.

By evening, it was all over. Constantine's army collected the bodies of the fallen. Those who had lost their shields searched for the victorious symbols. Maxentius's muddy body was found in a cluster of reeds. Rome had been taken.

And the next morning, his brawny chest covered with glittering armor, Constantine rode into the city, welcomed as a liberator. Behind him marched his army, waving a spear topped with the head of Maxentius.

In thanks to the Christian God for his victory at Rome, Constantine the Great signed the Edict of Milan, a law promising that the empire would never again persecute Christians for their faith. Christianity was finally legal.

EARLY CREEDS AND COUNCILS

THE FIRST COUNCIL of the ancient church is recorded in the Bible in Acts 15. A division between the Jewish and Gentile Christians brought the apostles to Jerusalem to decide what to do. When they agreed on a solution, they sent out a letter to all the churches with instructions.

After the deaths of the apostles, the task of defending the truth was left to new generations of Christians. More than once, powerful leaders in the church rejected the teaching of the apostles. These *heretics*, or "dividers," and their *heresy* sometimes became popular. To fight heresy, the church fathers followed the example of the apostles and called bishops together for a council, representing their local churches. Many such councils were held during the early church period.

When the council had made a decision, the bishops wrote a creed explaining the true doctrine and sent it to all the churches. The word *creed* comes from a Latin word that means, "I believe."

Within the first few hundred years of the church, most of the councils were held in response to false teachers who rejected the doctrine of the Trinity. The Bible teaches that there is God the Father, God the Son, and God the Holy Spirit—three persons, but one God. Many heretics, including a pastor named Arius and his followers, did not believe that Jesus and the Holy Spirit are God.

The first council to address this problem was held in the city of Nicea in 325 at the invitation of Emperor Constantine the Great. Under the leadership of Alexander of Alexandria, Nicea defended the deity of Jesus. The statement produced by the bishops at Nicea is now known as the *Nicene Creed*, one of the most famous creeds ever written.

But by the time the council had made their decision, the church was already deeply divided. For over fifty years, the fathers worked hard, even under threat of death, to heal the broken church. Finally, in 381, another council held in the city of Constantinople, led by Gregory of Nazianzus and Gregory of Nyssa, brought an end to Arianism.

Many other councils were held during the early years of the church. Some of the most famous are:

The Council of Ephesus (431) condemned the idea that Christ is two persons, one God and the other, man. The council argued that Christ is one person with two natures, one divine and the other human, which is important to a proper understanding of Jesus as God.

The Council of Chalcedon (451) gave the church an official statement explaining how Jesus is both God and man. Jesus had to be both God and man so he could save sinners, so this council helped the church better understand salvation.

The Councils of Carthage (397 and 419) affirmed the number of books in the Bible as we have them today.

Athanasius: Do martyrs die for a mere man?

362 AD. THE NILE RIVER, UPPER EGYPT.

LEANING OVER THE rail of the ship a short, dark-skinned man prayed silently, the breeze tugging at his white beard. As the boat moved forward, he gazed at the villages passing by on the banks of the Nile. Dusty-robed men prodded camels loaded with baskets and heavy bundles along the water's edge. Behind them, the green fields of the fertile river valley rolled out towards the great, brown cliffs of the desert.

"Old man!" shouted a soldier from an approaching boat.

The bearded traveler turned slowly.

"Have you seen Athanasius, the bishop of Alexandria? I know he is on the river somewhere. Has he passed by?"

It was hot under the scorching Egyptian sun, and the old man wiped beads of sweat from his forehead.

The soldier put his hand on the hilt of his sword. "I demand your cooperation in the name of the emperor!"

The traveler leaned forward and gazed at the soldier with steady black eyes. "You have almost caught up with him," he said slowly.

"Just row a little further."

The officer turned at once and shouted to his men. "Get this boat moving! The prisoner is just ahead of us."

Immediately, the ship bearing the emperor's insignia pulled ahead and was lost in the glare of the sun on the water. The old man heard a chuckle behind him.

"You are clever for an old bishop!" said the river captain, shaking his head.

The old man grinned. "I told him the truth. If he had boarded this boat, he could have arrested me."

"Emperor Julian should train his soldiers to ask more questions."

The bishop's smile disappeared. "Emperor Julian should not tempt God by exiling his bishops. I have spent my whole life preaching the gospel of Jesus. I am no threat to a young emperor."

"Don't worry, Bishop," the captain said, clapping Athanasius on the back. "Now that you've sent the soldiers on a detour, it won't be long until we get you into the protection of your friends."

"They should be used to hiding me by now! This has happened too often. It wastes valuable time I should be spending with my congregation in Alexandria." Then he smiled again. "But I do enjoy visiting my childhood friends in the desert."

After the captain left him, the old bishop kneeled on the warm deck to pray. The weathered planks were hard under his stiff knees, but he was grateful for his freedom. "Gracious Father," he prayed. "Thank you once again for preserving your humble servant."

He thought back to his early days in the desert. He had been born in one of the small villages on the Nile and grew up in a poor family. Because he was short and had dark skin, he earned the nickname "Black Dwarf." As a young man, he often sought refuge in the desert with the monks who lived there and cared for him like a son.

"Love God," they repeatedly taught. "Value truth. Learn to discipline your body and soul."

He was a bold young man with a fiery spirit and strong convictions about the teachings of the Bible. His teachers recommended him to Alexander, the great bishop of the Egyptian city of Alexandria. Alexander ordained him a deacon and made him his apprentice.

From the bishop, Athanasius learned how to burn incense, how to care for the poor, how to preach sermons, and how to serve communion. He was impressed with the bishop's strong convictions about Scripture.

Soon after Athanasius arrived in Alexandria, he learned that the bishop was involved in a public controversy. Alexander explained one day as they walked together to a hospital for the poor.

"As bishop," Alexander said, "it's my job to make sure that the people of the city are being taught the Bible. It is hard work that keeps me preaching, writing books, and training other church leaders like you."

"The people seem happy to have you as their bishop," Athanasius said. "They must be learning a lot from you."

Alexander sighed. "It is an honor to serve God here, but sometimes my duties are unpleasant. Recently I had to condemn the writings of a local presbyter named Arius, who claims that Jesus is just a man and not God."

The young man stopped walking and stared at the bishop. "If Jesus isn't God, why should we worship him? Do martyrs die for a mere man?"

"That is precisely the problem!" Alexander exclaimed. "It is a lie that corrupts the very foundations of Christianity. I have demanded that Arius stop teaching this doctrine."

"Has he stopped?"

"No." The bishop scowled. "Instead, he is challenging my authority. He wrote letters to the bishops of other cities defending his false teaching. Some of them now believe that he is right!"

They began walking again. "How can a Christian believe such a thing about Jesus?" Athanasius wondered. Distracted by his thoughts, he stepped into a pile of garbage in the street. He wrinkled his nose and scraped his sandal against a doorstep.

"These mistaken bishops are now teaching his ideas to their congregations and defending him," the bishop said, shaking his head. "The church is taking sides over this, Athanasius. There have even been riots in some cities of the empire!"

"Is there any way to stop this? God must be disturbed by such disorder in his church."

"The only way to stop false teaching is to preach the truth and ask God to give his people the hearts to believe that truth." He paused at the door of the hospital. "We can start with the people here that are sick and dying. Let's go in and pray with them."

Athanasius began to join Alexander in prayer, and the bishop kept preaching. But the controversy continued. Eventually, Emperor Constantine ordered Alexander and the other bishops to meet and settle the issue.

"We're going to hold a council of bishops in the city of Nicea to determine what the Bible really says about Jesus," Alexander told the young deacon. "You will go with me as my assistant."

In Nicea, Alexander preached every day and answered the questions of his colleagues. Only the bishops were allowed to attend the meetings, so each evening Athanasius waited in the courtyard for his mentor to come outside and tell him about the day's arguments.

They had been debating for many days when Alexander finally had good news. "We have done it!" he cried, shaking his apprentice by the shoulders. "God has opened the eyes of the bishops, and the majority has sided with us."

"What happens now?"

"Arius is banished from the empire and his teachings are officially declared unbiblical. Now we can get back to our work in Alexandria."

Some time later, Alexander fell very ill and called Athanasius to his bedside. "You have served me and the church well," he said with a weak smile. "When I am gone, you will be appointed the new bishop."

"I am not worthy of such a position," the young man insisted. "It is a lot of responsibility. I want a quiet life out of the spotlight."

"God has greatly gifted you, and he will require you to use those gifts. You are a bright and godly man, and the church needs leaders like you who will protect the truth."

The congregation agreed. When Bishop Alexander died, they convinced Athanasius to take his place.

The new bishop was popular with the people, but like his mentor, it didn't take him long to make a few enemies. Though Alexander had fought hard to prevent it, Arianism was becoming acceptable again in some parts of the empire. Athanasius knew that even if it made him unpopular, it was his job to remind the people what the Bible taught and what the bishops had declared about Jesus at Nicea. So he wrote several books against Arianism.

"An urgent message has arrived for you, sir," said his new assistant one day, handing the bishop a document sealed with wax.

Athanasius tore open the seal, shaking his head as he read. "This is ridiculous! The Arians are trying to disgrace me so people will stop reading my books. Someone started a rumor about me, saying I killed one of my opponents and cut off his hand!"

"Who would believe that about you?"

"Apparently some of the other bishops would. This is a summons to appear before them to answer the charges. Pack my things, Philip. I must leave at once and clear this up."

He made a detour on his journey and picked up another traveler.

On the appointed day, he entered the courtroom alone. The church officials sat before him in a half circle. He said nothing as he approached, but his alert eyes studied each of the witnesses. They were men he didn't trust.

"Bishop Athanasius," said the man in charge. "You are accused of murdering the teacher Arsenius and cutting off his hand to use for black magic. What do you have to say for yourself?"

"Sir," Athanasius replied with a respectful nod. "You accuse me of murdering Arsenius." From the back of the courtroom he brought forward a man wearing a hooded cloak. "Do you mean this Arsenius?" The bishop yanked off the hood, and everyone in the courtroom gasped.

"That's Arsenius!" someone said. "He's alive!"

The official in charge turned to the men who claimed to have witnessed the murder. They whispered furiously to each other.

"Very well," the judge said. "We can see that the teacher is alive. But perhaps you just cut off his hand."

Athanasius pulled up the man's sleeve. "Do you mean this hand?" The teacher's hand trembled nervously, but it was clearly still attached to his arm. The people in the room began to mumble.

"It was his other hand!" someone shouted.

Athanasius pulled up the other sleeve. "This man still has two hands!" He glared at the lying witnesses. "Did you think Arsenius was a monster with three hands?"

The courtroom broke into loud laughter. The judge glared at the witnesses and stood up from the table. "Bishop Athanasius, you are cleared of the charges against you," he declared. "Go in peace."

Athanasius hurried out of the building, anxious to return to his church. But as he walked, he realized that things were bound to get worse. "It's time I talked to the emperor about these false teachers," he thought. "Perhaps I should make the trip to Constantinople now." He headed for the capital of the empire.

The walls of Constantinople reached as far as Athanasius could see. Before Emperor Constantine had rebuilt the city and named it after himself, it had been a crumbling ancient town. But now as he walked through the capital, the bishop passed a number of ornate statues, blocks of beautiful houses, and several public baths where the people came to wash. The streets were full of artists carving sculptures and workers building houses, their hammers clattering against the stone. Everything was brand new.

He walked under a row of colorful canopies in the market, where merchants displayed their goods for sale. The air was heavy with dust and spices. "Fresh fish," the merchants called to him as he passed by. "Excellent vegetables, sir." "Would you like to buy some lovely pottery?"

Finally, Athanasius reached the palace and gazed in awe at the gleaming pillars. But once he got inside the gate, he was disappointed.

"I'm sorry," the imperial aid insisted. "Constantine the Great is much too busy to see you."

"Even Constantine must have time for the church," Athanasius argued. "Tell him that I am the bishop of Alexandria."

But when the aid returned, the answer was still the same. "The emperor cannot be disturbed."

Athanasius left the palace discouraged by his failure to arrange a meeting. He stopped at a market stall and bought a loaf of bread. "It isn't the emperor's schedule that kept you away," the merchant said, when Athanasius told him of his journey. "It is his advisor, an Arian teacher who is trying to keep the emperor from being influenced by non-Arians."

"This issue is even more urgent than I thought," the bishop realized. "I'll have to find another way of getting the emperor's ear, no matter what it takes."

He was heading back toward the palace gates when he noticed

two soldiers talking about Constantine. They hadn't seen him. He darted behind a pillar and listened.

"General Gaius keeps trying to talk him out of it," said one of the soldiers, "but you know the emperor. Every morning he saddles his horse and heads through this gate for a long ride in the countryside by himself."

"No one is swifter with a sword than the emperor."

"True. But it's still not safe for him to go out alone. You never know who might be waiting for him."

"That's it!" Athanasius thought. "Finally I'll be able to speak to him, away from his advisors."

It was still dark the next morning when he found a spot on the road just outside the city walls. He crouched under a bush for nearly an hour, waiting for the sound of approaching hooves.

There he is! A magnificent stallion galloped around a curve in the stony path, urged on by a rider in gleaming armor. In one quick motion the small bishop leaped out of the shrubs in front of the horse, grabbing the bridle as the horse reared.

Drawing his sword, the expert rider instantly brought the animal under control and forced his blade against the bishop's throat. "You dare to attack the emperor?" he cried.

The horse shook his head in protest, but Athanasius did not release his grip on the bridle. He looked at the emperor's tense muscles and the anger flashing in his dark eyes. "Mighty emperor," he said, standing his ground. "I mean you no harm. I am the bishop of one of your cities."

The emperor's eyes narrowed. Then he gave a short laugh and sheathed his sword. "Why would an educated man act so foolishly?" he demanded. "If I had been less careful, you would be headless now."

"And I am grateful for your hesitation, my lord," the bishop said boldly. "But I must speak with you and your guards will not admit me into your palace. Hear my case now, and I will leave you to ride in peace."

"You are a strange little man," Constantine said. "I will give you five minutes. What is so important that you hunt me like a wild boar?"

"The truth, my lord. That is most important."

When the bishop left him, the emperor returned to his palace and told his advisor of the meeting. "Why didn't you tell me he was trying to make an appointment to see me?"

"That bishop is a fanatic," insisted the Arian teacher. "A man who approaches you in this manner is dangerous."

"He wasn't carrying a weapon. But he was bold, and sincere about his concerns."

The advisor frowned and glanced about the room, trying to think of an excuse. "My lord, that bishop claims he is powerful enough to stop your shipments of wheat to Rome! He must be removed from leadership."

When Athanasius returned home, a messenger was waiting for him. "As punishment for your threats against the emperor, you are being exiled from Alexandria," he announced.

"What threats? I just had an audience with Constantine, and he said nothing about such a false accusation."

"Prepare to go. An escort will arrive tomorrow to make sure you leave."

He was not allowed to argue his case before the emperor. Forced to live far away from his home and his congregation, Athanasius kept preaching and writing about the truth of the gospel. While he was gone, the government of Alexandria appointed a new bishop named Gregory.

Word arrived that Constantine had died. Athanasius was allowed to return to Alexandria, but his homecoming was short. Both Athanasius and Gregory claimed to be the rightful bishop, and their supporters started a riot in the city. Constantine's sons, who had taken over the empire after their father's death, blamed Athanasius for the violence, and he was banished again. He longed to be back home. "If God wants me to do his work in Alexandria," he told himself, "then he will lead me back when the time is right."

A council of church leaders voted in favor of Athanasius, convincing the new emperors to return him to his place in Alexandria. Gregory had been such a poor leader that the people welcomed Athanasius as a liberating hero. For the next ten years he wrote and taught the truth in peace.

But the peace did not last. The bishop's assistant knocked at his door one day with a worried expression.

"What's wrong, Philip?"

"I'm sorry, Bishop. It's another imperial messenger with bad news."

"I'm getting tired of these visits! What does he want now?"

"Here, see for yourself." He handed Athanasius a message with the imperial seal.

"My request to see the emperor has been accepted?" The bishop raised his eyebrows. "I didn't ask to see him. This is a trick!"

"Constantine's son follows the counsel of his father's Arian advisors. He wants to get rid of you, but you are too popular to banish again."

Athanasius threw the parchment down on his desk. "Send a reply, Philip. Tell him it seems there has been an error. I did not request an audience with the great emperor and do not wish to waste his time with the simple talk of an old bishop."

Philip shook his head as he dipped his quill in an inkwell. "He will not like your response. May God protect you."

The bishop was serving communion at the church when a troop of soldiers surrounded the building. When their captain gave the order, they rushed in with a shout. "In the name of the emperor, hand over the bishop!"

The people panicked, running for the doors in confusion. The armed soldiers forced their way through the crowd toward the front of the church. But when they got there, the bishop was gone.

Outside, a carriage churned up dust as it pulled hastily away from the church.

"Where am I?" Athanasius blinked and leaned out of the carriage.

"You were helping people escape the soldiers when you fainted," said Philip. "In the chaos, we carried you outside. While the soldiers are busy questioning the congregation, we're taking you to the desert. You still have friends there, don't you?"

"They are always happy to see me," he nodded. "But for once I would like to visit them under different circumstances!"

"I wonder how long I will be there this time," he thought.

He stayed with the desert monks another five years, and spent most of his time writing more books. When Emperor Julian came to power, Athanasius was allowed to return to Alexandria.

"Arius is dead now, but the church is still debating his teaching. It is time for another church council, like the one my mentor Alexander attended years ago in Nicea," he declared soon after his return. "Invite all the bishops here, Philip. We must put this issue to rest."

Athanasius and the other bishops gathered in Alexandria for many days, studying the Bible together. Philip waited outside to get an update each night on their progress. Eventually, Athanasius emerged with a smile.

"You must have good news, bishop! What happened?"

"We are finally united. The bishops have agreed that the Bible teaches that God the Father, God the Son, and God the Spirit are three distinct persons but still one God."

"Then the followers of Arius must stop their false teaching now. This council is the most important thing you have ever done!"

But not everyone was happy about the outcome of the council. A short time later, Athanasius received a familiar message from Julian. An imperial refugee once again, he now sat on the deck of a ship, waiting for the current to deliver him back to the protection of the desert.

"The captain says we had a narrow escape!" said Philip, coming from below deck to join him.

Athanasius nodded. "God has preserved me again," he said. "I'm old and tired, but I have a feeling it won't be long before I'm back in Alexandria."

"Wherever you are, you'll be preaching the truth until your last breath."

"God is faithful, Philip. Though the enemy tries to stop us, the church of Christ just keeps growing."

They stood in silence at the railing and watched the sun slowly sink behind the desert cliffs on the horizon.

Athanasius did return to Alexandria, and spent his remaining years in peace, writing theology books. Despite the threats and exile he endured, he died of old age in his bed, surrounded by friends.

THE GREAT CAPPAD⊕CIANS: PERHAPS
Y⊕U HAVE NEVER ⅢET A BISH⊕P

370 AD. NICOMEDIA, ON THE BLACK SEA.

DESPITE THE RULING of the Nicene Council, Arian teachers continue to spread their beliefs throughout the empire. When Emperor Valens accepts the Arian doctrine, the situation becomes desperate for the orthodox bishops...

A weathered ship knocked against the dock where eighty bishops stood. Facing them, splendid in his gilded Roman armor, was Modestus, prefect of the emperor's personal Praetorian Guard. Behind him waited a contingent of the elite troops. They glanced at the darkening sky as thunder rumbled in the distance.

"This isn't right!" cried Bishop Urbanus. A stiff wind was rising off the sea, and he had to shout to be heard. "You invited all of us Nicene bishops here to debate with your Arian leaders, and instead you're exiling us? Doesn't Emperor Valens honor his word?"

Modestus shrugged. "The emperor changed his mind."

"There aren't any Arians here for us to debate! He didn't change

117

his mind. He planned this all along!"

Sneering, Modestus leaned closer to the bishop. "Valens is changing the face of the empire. The Nicene cause will soon perish, and the Arians will win."

"You'll never win," insisted Urbanus. "God is still in control, and he won't allow the truth to perish."

"You're right," snapped the prefect. "Fortunately, God is on our side." He ordered the soldiers to get the bishops aboard the ship.

"If he is on your side, then why not try us in public? Why are we being sent away secretly?"

Modestus ignored him. The veins in his neck bulging, he shouted, "Move! I want them on board before the weather gets too rough."

Prodded by imperial spears, the bishops boarded the rocking boat. Urbanus kept an eye on the prefect, who had pulled the ship's captain aside.

"Are we clear on the plan?" asked Modestus in a low voice.

"Yes," answered the captain. "When do I get paid for my loss?"

"When your duty is done. As soon as the boat is far enough out, the sailors are to lock the bishops in their cells and then burn it down."

"They still think they're being exiled?"

"Not for long," said Modestus with a grim smile.

The crew raised the anchor and hoisted the sails, moving out to the swelling sea. Modestus watched from shore as a flame began to lick at the rigging and then spread across the deck. A lifeboat full of sailors rowed back toward the dock. Modestus turned and led his troops away, as the cries of the trapped bishops reached the shore.

The heavy rains came too late to save them.

On a bright sunny day in the Cappadocian city of Caesarea, several presbyters stood talking in the doorway of the church. Lying between the northern waters of the Black Sea and the deep waves of the Mediterranean Sea, Cappadocia was a meeting point of all the main roads. News of the eastern empire came through Caesarea and into the church at the center of the city. "Emperor Valens is forcing Arianism on the bishops in Antioch," said Felix, a presbyter in Caesarea. "And he makes that dog Modestus do his dirty work."

"I think Modestus is happy to do the dirty work," replied a presbyter named Demetrius. "The prefect is a cunning man. When he gets involved, he does it to promote his own interests, not just to please the emperor."

"Ever since he murdered the bishops on that ship two years ago, everyone is terrified of exile. How do we know it's not a death sentence?"

"With the emperor planning to stop in Caesarea on his way to Syria, there is bound to be trouble here. But Valens and Modestus haven't dealt with Bishop Basil yet."

They were interrupted by a booming voice behind them. "Wouldn't your time be better spent praying for the emperor instead of gossiping about him?"

"Gregory of Nazianzus!" exclaimed Felix. "I didn't know you were in Caesarea. How is your father's church back home?"

"Strong, and my father is well," said Gregory. "Would you excuse me? I've had a long journey. Where may I find Basil?"

"He is over there with the dark-haired woman. We just buried her husband."

"Thank you." Gregory headed across the courtyard. The young woman was dabbing at her eyes and talking to a man of medium height who stood as straight as a pole. A breeze made the man's long beard dance. He had aged since Gregory saw him last, but his eyes were alert as ever. When he caught sight of his childhood friend coming toward him, he said a gentle good-bye to the woman and hurried to meet Gregory.

"How good it is to see you again!" said Basil, embracing his guest. "I'm so glad you came."

"How could I ignore your request?" Gregory replied with a smile. "Once the emperor arrives here, they will no doubt try to force you to accept Arianism. It's been a while since I joined you in a debate."

"You have not been to Cappadocia for some time."

"I was afraid if I showed up you would force me to be a bishop somewhere."

Basil looked at his friend in mock dismay. "Would I do that to you?"

"You did to your brother!"

The bishop's face was suddenly serious. "I was desperate, and there are few men we can trust to resist heresy these days," he said. "My brother Gregory is struggling in Nyssa. He hasn't been there long, and he is a private man who hates public service. The enemies of the gospel are already attacking. The emperor is using his Arian allies to accuse Gregory of things he hasn't done. I don't know yet what will come of it, but he is fighting the good fight."

"Well, I am here to fight, too. I will stay as long as necessary to debate the Arians, but I'm not here to get one of your 'promotions'!"

"Of course," agreed Basil, his eyes twinkling.

They went into the church and sat at the back of the sanctuary.

"You are in a powerful position here as bishop of Caesarea," said Gregory, "but the emperor's persistence is forcing many bishops to turn against Scripture."

Basil turned to him resolutely. "Many will give in, but the majority will not."

"Many have died for our cause, Basil, and you are as headstrong and outspoken as any. You must be careful."

"Indeed."

"But no more of this discouraging talk! You must have some good news to tell me. Have you heard from your sister? How is the Teacher?"

The nickname brought another smile to Basil's face. "Macrina is well," he answered. "The women of her monastery are serious about living a godly life. I have not seen her lately, but her faith is like iron."

"Our faith may soon be tested," said Gregory. "We would be greatly blessed if God grants us the strength of that woman."

They shared a meal before Basil returned to his room. Removing his sandals, he knelt on the hard floor and began to pray for his church, for his brother in Nyssa, and for the trials he knew he would soon face.

After an hour, he rose and pulled a small wooden box from behind his bed. Among the letters inside were several from Macrina that he saved for times when he needed encouragement. On top was one he read often.

"My dear brother," she had written, "do not care for the things of this life. Don't be turned by sympathy for them."

He replaced the letter in the box and stretched out on his hard bed, his arms folded over his chest. It had been a long time since he had seen her in Annesi, but images of his older sister stood firm in his memory. Her hair was gray now, her slim hands stained with years of hard labor in the monastery, but he had always believed her to be the most beautiful woman in the world. "I nearly wasted my youth seeking the praises of this world," he thought. "It was her strength and godliness that turned me to Christ."

Seeing his old schoolmate and reading his sister's words prompted a rush of childhood memories. He came from a wealthy Christian family. His educated father had taught Basil and his siblings languages and Scripture and rhetoric at home, until he died while Basil was still a boy. His mother moved from their home in Caesarea to their country estate in Annesi, but she sent Basil back to the city to finish school, and then to Athens. He had met Gregory of Nazianzus there.

When he came home to teach rhetoric in Caesarea, Macrina scolded him for being vain. By that time she had founded a community for women who wanted to spend their lives in prayer. He was still not used to seeing her plain clothes and simple life. His time was spent shining brightly in the academy and seeking a life of glory. He respected his sister, but he didn't see the need to follow her example.

"Basil, you are a brilliant man, but you think too highly of yourself," she told him when he returned from Athens. "Your gifts come from God, and you should give him the glory. Why don't you use your gifts for the church?"

"Becoming a famous teacher will honor the family name."

"Yes, but have you forgotten our heritage?" asked Macrina. "Our grandparents survived the persecution of Decius. Our grandfather was a martyr for the faith."

"I haven't forgotten what our mother taught us," he snapped, "but I am following the wishes of our father."

The conversation echoed in his head like it was yesterday. He remembered the shock he felt soon after, when he received word in his classroom that his brother Naucratius was dead. A hunting accident had cut short his life of dedication to the church. Basil began to reconsider his sister's warnings.

"It took my brother's death to teach me that my life belongs to God," he thought, closing his weary eyes. Macrina had welcomed him back to Annesi. Everyone called her the Teacher. On the banks of the River Iris, surrounded by mountain forests, she had taught him to trust God and to pray. His old schoolmate Gregory joined him there and together they founded a second monastery not far from his sister's.

"How different my life is now! I could never have known then that God would send me back to this city as bishop. It is so much work, but God will bless it," he told himself. "Soon the Nicene cause will prevail." He rolled on his side and drifted into a troubled sleep.

Many days passed. The city prepared to receive the emperor. Basil and Gregory held public debates with the Arians and spoke the truth to as many people as they could. One morning, they were praying in Basil's sunlit office when Demetrius burst in.

"Bishop! They've come for you!"

Basil came to his feet in surprise. "Who?"

"Modestus," said Demetrius, wringing his hands. "Apparently the emperor sent him ahead to interview you and see if you are going to cause trouble when he arrives."

"If he insists I stop teaching that Jesus is God, then he'd better believe I am going to cause trouble! When does he want to interview me?"

"An escort is here now, and they insist you return with them."

"Modestus has no authority over me or this church," Basil declared. "But it is an opportunity to speak the truth to my opponents. I'll go wherever God sends me," Basil said, striding towards the door. "It is his cause I defend."

"Wait," Gregory insisted. "I'm coming with you. But you must promise me something."

"Yes?"

"Whatever happens, we do not board any boats."

Basil grinned at his friend.

They were escorted from the church to a private chamber in the imperial court. Several men in church robes sat in a row at the front of the courtroom. Modestus paced before them, his footsteps ringing across the tiled floor.

"This is a private interview. You will wait outside," a guard said to Gregory as they entered.

"I'm here of my own will and not by any order," Basil insisted. "He is with me."

"He can stay until he opens his mouth," said Modestus behind him.

Basil left Gregory at the back and stepped forward. The prefect and the bishop eyed each other suspiciously.

Basil pointed to the clergymen. "I thought this was a private interview. Who are they?"

"They are bishops, and they will serve as witnesses to this discussion."

"They are Arians!"

Modestus gestured to a table. "Have a seat."

"I wish to remain standing."

"So be it," said Modestus, clasping his arms behind his back. "Haven't we met before? You came to me seeking tax relief for the Caesarean clergy."

Basil waved his hand impatiently. "Why am I here?"

The prefect gave him a haughty smile. "Fine. If you wish to be direct, I will be direct. Tell us, Basil, are you a supporter of the Nicenes?"

"If you are asking if I teach the creed of the Nicene council, then the answer is yes."

"Then you accept the Nicene position?"

Basil faced him with confidence. "I believe that Jesus is more than a man. He is fully God and fully man, not a created being as the Arians falsely teach."

"You will not be persuaded from this position?"

Basil folded his arms across his chest. "Why should I be? This is the teaching of Scripture, confirmed by the council of bishops who met at Nicea."

"The emperor and the bishops here today interpret Scripture differently."

"They are in error."

Modestus arched an eyebrow and sneered. "You dare to dishonor the beliefs of your emperor?"

"My true sovereign is God," said Basil carefully. "It is not his will for me to worship a created being. If Jesus is only a creature like me, I might as well worship myself!"

The Arian bishops began to whisper angrily.

"You go too far, Bishop. I don't think you realize the extent of my authority."

Basil raised his chin. "You don't have the authority of a church council. What can you do to me?"

"I have the authority of the emperor!" Modestus cried. "I can take everything you own, exile you, torture you, or kill you."

"Is that all? Those things don't scare me."

"Of course they do. Don't try to impress me with your false courage."

Basil stepped forward and looked straight into his interviewer's eyes. "You cannot take from me what I do not have, unless you want these tattered rags I wear and a few books. You cannot exile me, because every land belongs to God and I am his guest no matter where he takes me. And torture!" Basil threw his hands in the air with a laugh. "Torture is nothing. Torture is the friend who delivers me to my Savior in death."

Modestus clenched his fists. "No man speaks to me that way!"

"Perhaps you have never met a bishop." Basil glanced meaningfully at the silent witnesses.

In the corner, Gregory chuckled, until the guard put a hand on his spear in warning.

"If you met a bishop, this is what he would tell you," Basil continued, louder. "We love to serve our emperors and obey the law. That is what God commands us to do. But if the emperor—or his assassin—places himself higher than God, we will defy your fire, sword, or wild beasts. When the interests of God are at stake, we care for nothing else!"

Modestus stared at him, his mouth open in surprise. His informants had told him that this local bishop was a Nicene, and he planned to depose him after a brief interview. But Basil was more powerful than he expected. "This is not over," he declared. "The emperor will arrive shortly, and you can be sure he will have something to say." He shot a contemptuous look at the Arian bishops and stomped away. The bishops scurried after him.

Basil and Gregory were shown back to the street.

"You may be the first person who has ever stood up to that bully!" Gregory exclaimed when they were out of earshot.

"I don't think it did any good, though. He's not going to just go away."

"No, especially after you embarrassed him in front of the Arians. What do you think he and the emperor will try next?"

"I don't know, but they're not going to ignore Caesarea anymore. We're a target now."

Valens arrived in Caesarea with great ceremony. The people thronged the streets, hoping for a glimpse of the emperor in his carriage. During the first weeks of his visit, there were parades and feasts, but no word from the court against the Nicenes. The presbyters in Caesarea began to think he would overlook them. But the blow Basil expected came soon enough.

He had just dismissed a prayer meeting. The sun was going down, and the congregation hurried to get home before dark. The streets of any imperial city could be dangerous at night. Basil lingered to blow out the candles and say good night to the presbyters. When he stepped out into the cool evening air, he was greeted with a shout. "Bishop!"

It was a familiar, unpleasant voice. He turned around slowly. Modestus was waiting on horseback with several armed guards.

"Excuse me, Bishop," he said with polite disdain. "I have a letter for you."

"You're a delivery boy now?"

The prefect snarled and jumped off his horse, stepping quickly across the courtyard. "It's an order from Emperor Valens."

"For me? Are you sure?" replied Basil, pointing to himself. "There must be others who deserve the emperor's attention far more than I."

"I told you this wasn't over," Modestus said, shoving the parchment into the bishop's hand. "The emperor has decreed that you are to be exiled."

Demetrius stepped out of the church behind Basil. Lanterns appeared in the shadows as some of the congregation turned back in curiosity.

"The details are in the letter. Because the emperor is such a gracious man, you will have a few days to prepare." He leaned closer. "It looks like you'll get to keep your tattered rags and books after all."

Basil tucked the letter into his belt, smiled, and continued on his way. Modestus turned abruptly back to his horse, and the people scattered, their lanterns bobbing across the dark streets.

When the appointed day arrived, Basil said good-bye to Gregory, Demetrius, and the hundreds of people gathered outside the church.

"I will pray for you, as you pray for me," he called to them. He raised his hands in blessing. "God give you the courage and wisdom to worship him in truth."

"How dare the emperor do this?" someone cried.

"Emperors come and go," said Basil with a smile. "I will be back."

"Even the emperor cannot escape God's judgment," assured Gregory.

As the people pushed forward to touch their bishop, a carriage screeched to a halt beside the church. "I'm ready to go," Basil called out to a soldier on horseback.

"The emperor has changed his mind," said the soldier. "His son is terribly ill. You are ordered to the palace to pray for the boy's healing."

Basil looked at Gregory.

"This could be another of Modestus's tricks," Gregory whispered.

"It could be. But it could also be a marvelous work of God." He nodded to the soldier and climbed into the carriage. "Don't worry, Gregory," he called out the window as the horses were urged into a gallop. "The carriage is not on fire!"

At the palace, Basil was rushed to the emperor's private apartments. Valens was dressed regally, but wore the haggard look of a worried father.

"He seems to have improved just since I sent for you," the emperor said, rising from his couch. "Will you pray for him?"

"Let me see him first."

He was led into the child's room. When the doctors stepped aside to let him pass, he was surprised to see a line of Arian bishops standing before the bed.

"Why are they here?" he demanded.

One of the bishops held a basin of water. "We are ready to baptize the child before he dies."

Basil glared at him, and then at Valens. "You would baptize your son as an Arian, yet you bring me here to call down God's healing?"

"I take no chances with my son's life." The emperor folded his arms across his chest.

Basil waved the bishops away and approached the bed. The child was pale, and shaking with fever. He leaned over the bed and took the child's hand in his. "Father," he prayed silently, "Valens is an enemy of your church, but this boy is just a child. There is still hope that he will serve you one day. If it be your will, restore him to health even now."

Then he turned back to the emperor. "God struck down Pharaoh's firstborn because he would not let Israel go. Now God has brought this calamity upon you because you have killed his faithful ministers. As long as you continue to defy the truth and harm the church, your house will feel God's anger."

The boy moaned. Valens put a trembling hand over his eyes. "Take Basil home," he ordered.

Basil walked out of the room. But when he reached the door, he turned back and saw that the bishops had surrounded the bed. He met the emperor's weary eyes. "To side with the Arians is to bring death to your house," he declared quietly.

The guards carried him out.

But he was stopped by a soldier before he reached the street. "There is sickness in the palace, Bishop," he said. "Your presence is requested."

"I've already been there, soldier," Basil replied. "I'm sorry that the emperor's son will not survive." He turned to go.

"No, sir," said the soldier, gripping Basil's shoulder. "Not the emperor's son. It's Modestus, prefect of the Praetorian Guard. He begs you to come pray for him."

"Modestus is ill?"

"Very ill, sir. Please come with me."

He led the way to the prefect's apartments. Modestus was lying in his bed, shivering like the child Basil had just seen.

"Why don't you call your Arian friends?" Basil said coldly. "They are still here sacrificing Pharaoh's firstborn."

"Please, Bishop!" Modestus cried, raising his head with great effort. "I am near death, and I have repented of my sins."

There was a sincerity in his voice that made Basil step closer.

"Basil, you have won your argument. Only grant me recovery."

Moved, the bishop knelt at his bedside, and prayed that God would heal this man who had been his enemy.

Gregory greeted Basil with relief when he returned to the church, and listened with amazement to his report. But they were saddened the next day when word arrived that Valens's son was dead. "If only he had not mingled salt water with fresh," Gregory said, "and invited you and the Arians to his bedside, perhaps God would have answered your prayer."

The empire was quiet for several weeks.

"Is it true that Modestus has recovered?" Demetrius asked Basil.

"That is what I am told."

"In his grief, Valens is staying out of the public eye," Gregory said. "Rumor has it that he regrets having allowed the Arians to baptize his son. He seems to have backed down from forcing the Nicene bishops to accept Arian teachings."

"We'll see if it lasts. In the meantime, we have lost a good many bishops who need to be replaced." He looked at Gregory.

"I have some reading to do," Gregory said, rising. "Excuse me."

Basil stood. "We need you at Sasima, Gregory. You know we need an orthodox bishop there."

"I am not qualified for such a position," Gregory insisted. "I said no, and I mean no." His hasty footsteps clattered down the hall.

"I think that's a no," Demetrius said.

Basil looked at the empty doorway. "He'll go to Sasima. He has devoted as much to the cause of truth as I have, and he knows we need him. But I'm afraid our friendship may become a casualty of this battle."

Basil was right. Gregory became Bishop of Sasima at Basil's insistence, but it caused a division between the two friends that lasted until Basil's death. Basil died in 379, and Macrina followed not long after. Gregory of Nyssa and Gregory of Nazianzus carried on as leaders of the Council of Constantinople in 381, which outlawed Arianism. Macrina, Basil (often called Basil the Great), Gregory of Nyssa, and Gregory of Nazianzus became known to history as the Great Cappadocians, defenders of orthodox Christianity.

Ambrose: A bishop cannot give up the temple of the Lord

374 AD. MILAN, A RESIDENCE OF THE IMPERIAL FAMILY.

THE DEATH OF Emperor Jovian ten years earlier caused the empire to again split into east and west. The Arian controversy continues, now influenced by two emperors...

"Governor, I fear the election will turn into a riot!"

The governor sighed and ran a hand over his round, balding head. "Auxentius has been dead for weeks and he's still making trouble."

"The outcome of this election is critical to both sides, sir," Paulinus reminded his superior.

"Yes, yes. Bishop Auxentius kept the Arians happy for twenty years, and now the Nicenes are ready to put one of their own back in the church," Governor Ambrose said, rising from the pile of legal documents on his desk. "I understand the controversy, of course, but I can't allow the dispute to give way to an unpleasant disturbance."

"Of course not, sir."

"Well, then, grab my cloak, Paulinus. Perhaps I can persuade my citizens to get through the election peacefully."

A throng buzzed outside the Basilica Portiana, the main cathedral in Milan. Children weaved in and out of a group clamoring to enter the ornate stone façade. Paulinus led the governor to a nearby regiment of soldiers ready to enforce order.

"A number of Nicenes are inside, trying to nominate their candidate," General Cassius said, acknowledging the governor with a quick bow. "The Arians insist that this is their church and are furious that their opponents have dared to cross the threshold. Come on, I'll get you inside." With a hand on the hilt of his sword, he cried, "Make way for the governor! Make way for Governor Ambrose!"

Inside, the debate was even more animated. The presbyters serving as election officials were surprised to see the governor. He was not an officer of the church.

"People of Milan," Ambrose called out, hand raised. He climbed the half dozen low steps at the front of the cathedral and stood in the chancel before the altar. "Hear your governor!"

The crowd hushed, glancing at the election officials suspiciously.

Ambrose clasped his hands behind his back and smiled benevolently. "Milan is an important city, and therefore, so is her bishop. Do not disgrace your city or your church with violence, but elect your bishop with peace and wisdom. Let each of you vote as you believe God would have you to do."

The Arian majority began to murmur. "The right of succession is ours," they complained to each other in low voices. "Can the governor allow the Nicenes to participate?"

Gesturing to the officials to resume the election, his governor's ring glittering on his hand, Ambrose began to descend the steps.

"Ambrose for bishop!" shouted a child above the disgruntled whispers.

The governor snapped around in surprise.

"Yes!" called one of the Nicene dissidents. "He is the only candidate that can reunite our city!"

Ambrose turned back, hands lifted high.

"Silence! I am no bishop. I am your governor!"

An Arian presbyter pushed forward. "If the Nicenes are allowed to participate, we may not get our candidate in," he urged his cohorts. "But if we elect Ambrose, we can at least keep their candidate out!"

"Ambrose, bishop!" The Arians picked up the cry. "Ambrose, bishop!"

"Nonsense!" Ambrose shouted. "Return to your election peacefully!"

The chant swelled, the people waving and stomping.

"I believe the people have made their choice, sir," yelled a smug presbyter.

"This way, Governor," Cassius called. "You'll never get through the front door." He led Ambrose and Paulinus to an exit at the left of the chancel. They shoved the heavy wooden door shut, muffling the uproar on the other side, and fled down the stairwell. At the bottom, Ambrose fixed Paulinus with an annoyed look. "This is not what I had in mind!"

They were spotted as soon as they stepped outside, and the crowd fell into pursuit. Outside the governor's residence, with Ambrose safely inside, they continued to chant. General Cassius posted soldiers at the gates just to be safe.

"This is ridiculous!" Ambrose bellowed, throwing up his hands and glaring at the election official standing opposite him.

"The election is legitimate, sir." The young presbyter twisted his cloak with nervous hands. "We've already notified the emperor.

It was our duty to turn over the results."

"You're dismissed." Ambrose glared at him. "Paulinus!"

The presbyter backed out the room, bumping into the governor's assistant, and fled with a mumbled apology.

Paulinus stepped forward. "Yes, sir?"

"Tell the stable master to prepare my horse. I think it's wise to leave Milan for a few days until this bishop nonsense blows over."

An hour later, Ambrose pulled a heavy cloak around his shoulders and led the mare through the dark stable yard, sidestepping a fresh pile of manure. Turning right at the gate, he nodded to a soldier at his post. The horse's iron and leather "hippo sandals" click-clacked quietly on the empty street.

"Halt!"

Ambrose turned the horse patiently. "At ease, soldier. You may not have recognized me in the dark. Maintain your post."

"I know who you are, Governor," said Cassius, stepping out of the shadows.

"General! I appreciate your personal protection, but as you can see, the mob has gone home for the night. You should get some rest. I expect a report when I return from my business."

Cassius took a step forward. "I can't let you do that, sir. I'm under orders from the emperor."

"What's this about?"

"The emperor doesn't want an Arian bishop, and he knows you're not as neutral in this debate as you appear. Allowing the Nicenes to participate tipped your hand, sir."

"I was simply enforcing a fair election."

"Yes, sir. However, the emperor has approved your election, and he suspected you might try to get out of it."

"Are you arresting me?"

"Not arresting, sir. Just supervising your compliance to the emperor's command. A messenger will be at your door any moment with orders for you to appear before the council of bishops for ordination."

"I am no bishop!" Ambrose said in exasperation. "I haven't even been baptized!"

"You're to be baptized on Sunday."

"I wasn't looking for a career change." He dismounted, and the mare nuzzled him curiously as they turned back toward the gate. "But I take my work seriously, Cassius. If the emperor wants me to be bishop instead of governor, I will do it to the best of my ability."

Eight days later, a consecration service at the cathedral declared him the new bishop of Milan. Simplicianus, a Nicene presbyter several years older than Ambrose, tutored him in the Scriptures. He spent his nights praying for wisdom and writing sermons. And the new bishop became more popular and more powerful than he had been as governor.

A steady stream of visitors passed through his church office. Old and young confessed their sins. The poor sought to pray with him. Government officials came for advice. Every Sunday, visitors from all over the empire jostled with the citizens of Milan in the cathedral, anxious to hear the bishop preach and be baptized by him. When the emperor died, Ambrose comforted the grieving citizens, including the widowed empress Justina and her son Valentinian. Setting up their imperial court in Milan, they listened to his sermons from a private pew at the front of the sanctuary.

"Watch your step," Simplicianus warned the bishop. "Our empress is Arian, and she is becoming more and more vocal in supporting the Arian bishops."

"Just because she has the power of the court behind her doesn't mean she's right," Ambrose replied. "I'll oppose her if I have to."

The bishop and the empress soon become public adversaries. Justina ordered him to set aside one of the churches in Milan for

Arian worship. Ambrose refused.

"A bishop cannot give up the temple of the Lord!" he declared before the royal court.

But the argument was interrupted by a protest outside the palace. Ambrose's congregation had heard of his imperial summons.

"Why hasn't the army brought this rabble under control?" the empress demanded.

Cassius dropped to one knee before the court and glanced at Ambrose. "Your eminence, when we tried to arrest them, they said they were willing to die for their cause!"

Valentinian shifted uneasily in his throne and turned to Ambrose. "Your congregation is a bit carried away, Bishop. Perhaps you should settle this."

Ambrose exited the palace and stood before the people. "Enough!" he shouted to the mob. "I assure you that no one will invade a cathedral of the church." The crowd cheered and carried Ambrose away.

"That was a dangerous move," Paulinus said later to Ambrose. "You've just proved that you have more influence over the people than the imperial court. Praise God for protecting you!"

"I'm going to need his continued protection," the bishop replied. "The empress will not give up so easily."

The following spring, Justina issued an edict demanding that Ambrose hand over another cathedral for an Arian celebration of Easter. He sent a letter, refusing to comply.

On Palm Sunday he argued his case in a sermon. "Jesus said to give to Caesar what is Caesar's, but give to God what is God's. The palace is the emperor's domain, but the church is the bishop's domain," he insisted. "The emperor is within the church, not over the church."

"Amen!" the congregation agreed.

A shout rose from the far corner, near a window.

Paulinus ran to the bishop with news. "Soldiers have surrounded the cathedral!"

The people snatched their children behind them and huddled together in prayer. Ambrose called Simplicianus forward and asked him to read a psalm. Slipping out of the side exit, he hurried through the damp chamber, pulling his wool mantle closer across his shoulders. Reaching the bottom of the stairs, he peered expectantly around the corner.

Cassius was waiting in the shadows.

"I knew I would find you here," the bishop said.

"And I knew you would come," the general replied.

"I came to pray for your soul, Cassius. What are you doing here? You oppose the Arian heresy. You must not betray the truth at any cost!"

"My soul is not in danger, friend. I have vowed my loyalty to the imperial family, but my first loyalty is to God. I will not allow his bishop to be injured while the empress steals his cathedral!"

"Doesn't that leave you in a difficult position?"

The general grinned. "I have strictly obeyed my empress. I am not to take the church by force, but surround it until you give up. Anyone can enter, but no one is allowed to leave."

"Well then, we'll have to outlast the empress. You're in for a long wait, general."

"My troops are up to the challenge! God be with you, Bishop."

The church lay under siege for several days. Ambrose wrote hymns and taught them to the people. Singing gave them a sense of unity against their opponents, and kept their minds off the sword-bearing soldiers outside.

"Let's try the last one again," the bishop was saying when soldiers burst into the sanctuary on the fifth day.

The people screamed and ran for cover. But the soldiers waved empty hands.

"We're not here to fight!" they proclaimed. "We've been ordered to break off the siege and our regiment is leaving. But we have come for the bishop's blessing."

Ambrose pronounced the blessing they desired. The relieved congregation praised God for his protection and returned to their homes.

The empress had no more opportunities to clash with the bishop. A short time later, Italy was invaded by a rival to the throne. The now seventeen-year-old emperor and his mother fled to Thessalonica. After the attack was defeated, they returned to Milan, but before long Justina died. Valentinian took his army to Gaul, to oversee his territories on the Rhine. Theodosius, emperor in the eastern part of the empire, came to Milan for an extended stay, and spent his Sundays in the front row of Ambrose's cathedral.

Ambrose and Simplicianus were sitting in the bishop's study, a summer breeze stirring the dust in the open latticework at the window. They were working intently on plans for a new church outside the city walls when they heard rapid footsteps echoing in the chamber outside. Paulinus rushed in, nodding respectfully but impatiently.

"I beg your pardon, Bishop."

"What is it, Paulinus?"

"Word has reached Milan. There's been a massacre in Thessalonica!"

The bishop and the presbyter rose in alarm. "A massacre! What happened?"

"Well, sir, Thessalonica has been housing imperial troops for some months now, ever since the attack on Milan. Apparently there was a dispute between General Butheric and a popular charioteer in the circus. Butheric had him thrown in jail, and the fans rioted. Butheric was killed. The military retaliated, striking down all the fans they could find. As many as 7000 are dead!"

"7000!" Simplicianus sank back on his bench.

Paulinus leaned toward Ambrose and looked at him gravely. "Sir, the people are saying that Emperor Theodosius ordered the retaliation."

Simplicianus squeezed his eyes shut and shook his gray head. "Even if he didn't, it is his army. He is responsible."

"He is scheduled to return soon from his trip," Paulinus remembered suddenly. "Aren't you supposed to be at the arrival celebration?"

"I am expected to be there with other leading citizens to welcome him back on behalf of the church, but——." The bishop squared his shoulders and clasped his hands behind his back. "I cannot allow a murderer into the church until he repents, not even the emperor."

"Sir, on his first Sunday back he will certainly expect to take communion," Paulinus said quietly. "What will you do?"

Ambrose was decisive as usual. "Prepare to deliver a letter to the palace. I must urge him to repent, and a private letter will be much better received than a public confrontation."

His companions left the room, exchanging worried glances. Ambrose returned to his desk and began to scratch away at a parchment.

My lord, he wrote, after the required introductory flattery, *the casual extermination of your own people is a severe sin which cannot be overlooked. It is no surprise that a man should sin, especially a man with such great gifts and temptations as yourself. But it is much worse if he does not admit his sin and humble himself before God. I plead with you to be reconciled with your Savior. Until you repent publicly, I cannot allow you to set foot on the sacred ground of the cathedral.*

Paulinus reported that the court had noticed the bishop's absence at the celebration. "Your letter was delivered directly to the emperor's assistant," he said. "The servants say Theodosius is in a bad temper."

"We must wait and see if God will change his heart," Ambrose said firmly.

For weeks, there was no reply from the emperor. Every Sunday during the bishop's sermon, Paulinus cast restless glances at the cathedral door. But the emperor did not appear.

"He will come eventually," Simplicianus said. "He cannot allow his people to believe he has turned his back on the church. But whether he will repent, well, that remains to be seen."

The next Sunday, the bishop was reading his Old Testament text when the cathedral doors were flung open. Theodosius stood in the entrance, his attendants behind him. A whispered murmur ran through the worshipers.

Ambrose descended the steps at the altar and stood with his right hand raised, his piercing eyes gazing steadily down the long aisle at the emperor. The tall candles at the front of the sanctuary flickered in the draft from the open door.

The bishop's voice rang out with authority. "A man whose hands are bathed in the blood of injustice is unworthy, until he repents, to enter this holy place and to take communion."

The emperor took a step forward. "Even Israel's greatest king David was guilty of murder."

"You have followed David in sinning. Now follow him in repentance."

The congregation followed the exchange in anxious silence.

Theodosius removed his imperial robe and let it drop at his feet. Dressed only in a simple tunic, he came forward and sank to his knees before Ambrose, his dark head bowed.

"I have committed this sin, Bishop Ambrose, and I come now in repentance, asking Christ to forgive me." He looked up at Ambrose, his eyes shining with tears.

The bishop raised his hands above the emperor. "God forgives those who ask for his mercy. Rise in peace, my lord."

The emperor got to his feet. "From now on," he declared in a loud voice, "if I decree that someone shall be put to death, the execution will be delayed for thirty days to ensure that I do not act out of wrath."

Moved to tears, the congregation began to call out praises to God.

Theodosius picked up his robe, adjusting it around him again, and took his seat at the front of the church. Ambrose climbed the steps and, with one finger, found his place in the Old Testament reading.

Paulinus leaned over to Simplicianus and whispered, "How many emperors can our bishop tame?"

The old presbyter smiled. "The heart of the king is like a river, said David in his psalms, and God can turn it in whatever direction he wills."

Ambrose preached at the funerals of both Valentinian II (393) and Theodosius (395). Best known for his original hymns and his stand against Arianism, he died peacefully on Good Friday, 397. His assistant Paulinus was commissioned by Augustine of Hippo to write The Life of Ambrose.

AUGUSTINE: OUR HEARTS ARE RESTLESS UNTIL THEY REST IN YOU

371 AD. THAGASTE, NORTH AFRICA.

STARS WINKED IN the sky above the outskirts of the small North African town of Thagaste. It was a clear night. Nestled in the valley between forests, most of the town's residents were farmers, including a councilman named Patrick. His was one of the larger farms, and had a reputation for the juiciest fruit in Thagaste. During the day, fields bustled with harvesters and shepherds. But once the sun set, the family and their servants went to bed, leaving the owls and insects to roam the dark pastures.

On this night, a group of teenagers brushed aside tree branches, tiptoeing through the orchard toward the farmhouse. A volley of pebbles against his window shutters startled a young man asleep in his bed. "Augustine!" came a loud whisper. "Come to the window."

He swung open the shutters, and the sudden cool breeze on his face woke him fully. Below his second story window, moonlight gleamed against the pale stones around the house. Gazing up at him on the other side were his friend Meandus and two girls he didn't recognize.

"Come down," Meandus called in a loud whisper.

Augustine threw his cloak over his shoulders and smoothed his hair. "Hang on." He slipped quietly out of the house and jumped over the stone wall. The girls smiled at him.

"This way," Meandus said, tugging on his friend's sleeve. "We're going to Villicus's orchard to get some pears." He set off across the field.

Augustine ran after him. "Don't you have your own fruit?"

"Yeah, but that's not the point." Meandus rolled his eyes in the dark.

"Why don't you steal from your next-door neighbor instead of mine?"

Meandus stopped and turned. "Are you afraid you're going to get caught?"

The girls laughed. "I thought you said your friend was fun," taunted one. "He's just a timid little boy."

Augustine squared his shoulders and glared at them in the dark. "I'm a man. I can do anything I want."

"Then let's go!" Meandus said, breaking into a run.

They crept over the neighbor's wall and found a pear tree. Augustine knew he could eat as much of his father's fruit as he wanted, but with the pretty girls at his side, he suddenly wanted this tree instead. "What are you waiting for?" he called.

They filled their cloaks with the plump, fragrant fruit. With each step in the damp grass, Augustine felt his blood rising with excitement. Their bundles heavy, they dashed back through the darkness to Patrick's farm.

"Over here," Augustine said, pointing to the pig pen. "The pigs will eat well tonight."

"Aren't you going to eat these?" Meandus asked.

Augustine shrugged. "My dad's pears are better." He swung up onto the fence next to one of the girls and threw pears to the pigs. They laughed as the animals grunted, lurching forward to get their share.

From an upper window in the house, a silent figure watched. He folded his arms across his chest and sighed in the shadows.

His wife rolled over in bed and sat up. "Patrick? Did something wake you?"

"Friendship can be a dangerous enemy, Monica," Patrick said, walking away from the window. "Augustine is almost seventeen. He's a man now! It is time for him to leave the farm. If we don't send him to Carthage soon, he'll never become a lawyer."

"What has he done now?"

He sat next to her on the edge of the bed. "It's nothing to worry about. But I had a conversation with my colleague Romanianus today. He wants to become Augustine's patron and pay for him to go to law school."

"I have tried to raise him as a good Christian," insisted Monica. "He is just too interested in having fun right now."

"Maybe your religion isn't what he needs," said Patrick, climbing back into bed.

"It is what he needs, but not what he wants."

"What he needs is to get a law degree in Carthage."

"I guess I'm afraid to send my boy away," Monica said with a sigh. "But he does need to begin a career. Tomorrow I'll start making preparations. Go back to sleep, Patrick."

Patrick kissed the top of her head and rolled over. "I hope the pigs aren't sick in the morning," he thought.

Augustine was not eager to leave his friends, but he soon discovered that he loved the sights and sounds of the big city. Carthage, a port on the Mediterranean Sea, was a cauldron of temptations. He soon rejected Christianity, exchanging it for the teachings of Mani, a philosopher who claimed he was the Holy Spirit. Augustine threw himself into his law studies, but spent his free time with his new classmates tramping through the marketplace, looking for trouble.

"Get your fresh apples!" yelled a vendor, carrying a basket on his shoulder. A gang of dirty children rushed past him, knocking his basket over. Augustine and his friends stood on the street corner and laughed as the merchant shook his fists.

Augustine looked at the fruit strewn across the market stall and thought of his father's farm. "I can't believe it's been three years since I left," he thought.

A string of colored glass beads twirled in a curtained doorway, catching his eye. He forgot about Thagaste. "Our favorite astrologer is open today," he said, stepping across the street. "Let's go get our palms read."

One of his friends ran after him and pulled him away. "We don't have time," he said. "The lecture starts in a few minutes. Besides, I thought you were following the Manichean religion now, not astrology."

"John, haven't you learned anything at law school?" said Augustine, jabbing his friend in the side. "I live by Cicero's motto: Find truth wherever it can be found."

"Your mother would not be happy with you, young man," mocked John in a nagging voice, his hands on his hips.

"She won't be happy with Amica either," said Augustine, frowning. He looked at the beautiful young woman waiting for him on the corner. Her long, dark hair and bronze skin were a constant distraction.

"Does your mother know about her?"

"I wrote to her, but I didn't say much. Since it's illegal for me to marry Amica because she's from a lower class, I didn't know how to explain our relationship to my mother."

He stopped behind the fruit vendor's stall and snatched up one of the fallen apples, slipping it into the leather pouch at his waist. The vendor was busy with a customer.

"And what about your other surprise?" asked John, as they walked back toward their friends. "Will she accept Adeodatus?"

"I'll have my degree soon, and then Amica and I will return to Thagaste. When my mother sees our son, her heart will melt." He put his arm around Amica, who held a sleeping infant close to her chest. "What woman doesn't love her grandson?"

"Come on," John said. "We're going to be late for the lecture."

The friends set off toward the forum, aware that their careless days together would soon be over.

It was a bright blue day in Thagaste when Augustine returned. Fields of bold African flowers rippled in the breeze. With Adeodatus tucked safely under his arm, Augustine led Amica toward the old homestead, pointing out the landmarks he remembered so well.

A familiar figure waved at them from a distance. "It's Meandus!" Augustine said. "We were best friends before I left for Carthage."

"Augustine!" cried Meandus, catching up with them. "You're back in Thagaste?"

"It's good to see you," said Augustine, embracing his friend. "It's been a long time since you convinced me to steal pears."

Meandus laughed. "I hear you've been busy since then. You're a lawyer now?"

"I'm better at public speaking, so I teach rhetoric to law students."

"And who is this?" He rubbed the dark-haired, little head in Augustine's arms, and nodded at the lovely woman beside him.

Augustine smiled proudly at Amica. "This is Adeodatus, our son. So much has changed since we last talked, Meandus. Let's meet in town tomorrow."

"I'll find you. See you then!" He waved as he ran off.

They continued toward the house. It was just as he remembered it, except for a few more weeds in the garden. He handed Amica the baby and reached for the door, but it flew open before he touched it.

Monica stood in the doorway. She was still young, but he noticed a few gray hairs along her temples and worry lines around her mouth.

"Oh, my son!" she cried, throwing her arms around him. Her tears soaked through his tunic.

"I'm back, Mother."

She released him and stepped back, wiping her eyes. "I have missed you. It is so good to see you, though you have broken my heart."

"I'm sorry that I didn't write more often, but I can make it up to you. I want you to meet someone." He drew Amica forward.

Monica glanced at the woman and her child, then turned back with sad eyes. "I'm sorry, Augustine. I know you want me to be happy for you, but I can't! You know this is a Christian household, and yet you bring your girlfriend's child and your false religion here as if nothing was wrong."

"You will love Amica when you get to know her," he declared. "And this is your grandson, Adeodatus."

"It was a mistake for you to come," she said quietly, turning away. "I cannot let you stay here."

He threw his hands in the air. "Mother, I will be teaching rhetoric in Thagaste. Surely you don't want your grandson to be homeless!"

"You have brought disgrace to this family!" she cried, choking back her sobs. "You didn't even show up for your father's funeral. If your brother hadn't been here, I would have buried him alone!"

"I received your letter, but I couldn't leave my studies."

"When will you grow up?" she demanded. "When will you

learn to think of others besides yourself?"

"Mother, please," he begged. "This is my home, too. Father would have welcomed me."

She looked away in silence. "It would be un-Christian to turn away someone in need," she said finally. "You can stay in the guest room for now." With that, she strode off toward the barn.

Amica stared after her, and Adeodatus began to cry. Augustine led them inside. "I'm sorry," he said.

"You shouldn't have shocked her like that," Amica replied, hushing the baby.

"I'll apologize and everything will be fine," he assured her.

But Monica avoided them, and refused to call Adeodatus her grandson.

Word spread throughout Thagaste that Augustine was home to teach rhetoric. Soon he had a classroom full of students. Meandus often slipped into the back to hear his friend lecture. Sometimes the discussion wandered into religion. Meandus was intrigued by Augustine's description of Manicheanism.

One night they had dinner together and sat outside on a hill in the dark, enjoying some relief from the daytime heat. Thunder rumbled faintly in the distance.

"You and I were brought up to be Christians," Meandus said. "You have rejected the teachings of the church, but I'm not sure I can do that."

"They are mere superstition. There is no shame in leaving them behind now that you see the truth of the Manicheans."

A bolt of lightning streaked across the sky above the mountains.

"I'd better get home before this storm arrives," Meandus said. "See you tomorrow?"

"Meet me after class."

The next day, Augustine waited for his friend, but he never

arrived. "Something must have come up," he thought. "I promised Adeodatus I'd play with him tonight anyway."

But two more days went by with no sign of Meandus. Augustine let his class out a few minutes early and dropped by his friend's house. The young man's mother answered the door with red-rimmed eyes.

"What's wrong?" he asked. "Is Meandus here?"

"He's very ill," she said, wringing her hands. "I can't wake him. The doctor arrived a few minutes ago."

He rushed to his friend's side. Meandus lay pale and motionless in his bed, his hair sticking to his damp forehead.

"How long has he been like this?"

"He came home with a fever two nights ago after being caught in a storm, and he's been asleep ever since."

He looked at the doctor, who shook his head.

There was another knock at the door, and Meandus's mother left the room. When she returned, the bishop of Thagaste was with her.

Augustine looked at her with surprise. She lowered her eyes.

"We are having him baptized," she said. "I want him to die a Christian."

Augustine drew a deep breath. He remembered a time when he was a boy, near death, and his mother had almost baptized him. "I'm glad I didn't accept Christian baptism since I don't believe in it anymore," he thought. "I doubt if Meandus would want it either, but I have no right to object to the beliefs of his family."

He said nothing, and the bishop baptized Meandus in his bed.

Augustine stayed at his friend's side the whole night. He had stepped outside for some fresh air when he heard a shout in the house and dashed back inside.

Meandus sat up in bed, embracing his relieved mother. He looked at Augustine. "Mother says that the bishop baptized me," he said with a weak voice. "God was warning me about rejecting him, Augustine. I should not have listened to you."

Augustine stared at his friend. "So it's my fault you got sick?"

"No, no, of course not. But I will repent for rejecting the Bible. Please do not say anymore to me about your Manichean beliefs." He leaned back on his bed, exhausted.

"If that is your wish," Augustine said.

He left the house and stalked back to the farm. "He'll get over this, and then we'll laugh about the baptism," he told himself.

He returned to his classes. For several days, there was no word from Meandus. "He must still be in bed repenting for his sin," he thought with irritation.

Then the news came. The fever had returned. Meandus was dead.

Augustine fell into a deep darkness. Every day he expected Meandus to show up after class, only to be reminded that he was gone.

"If I believed in Jesus, I would blame him for this," he thought, clenching his fists. In anger, he packed up his family to leave Thagaste for good.

"You can't run from God," Monica reminded him gently. "He's calling you to leave the Manicheans, not Thagaste. If you ever wish to see Meandus again, you must become a Christian."

"I love you," Augustine told her, "but I can't embrace your myths. I'm sorry. I'm returning to Carthage."

They left at daybreak.

In Carthage, he spent seven years teaching rhetoric. His class met in a three-sided porch in the center of town, divided from the bustling marketplace by only a heavy curtain. The students liked their young, brilliant teacher and they often stayed after class to learn more about his religion. But Augustine was not happy.

"What's wrong?" Amica asked him one night after Adeodatus

had gone to bed. "I haven't seen you smile for a long time, and you barely ate tonight."

He rubbed his eyes. "My students are rowdy and I'm getting tired of them. I don't enjoy teaching here anymore. Maybe it's time to leave."

"Leave Carthage? But this is our home!"

"My friend Alypius has gone to Rome, and he says there are many opportunities there."

"Rome is far from here."

"I have to think of my career, Amica. I'm never going to become the most famous rhetoric teacher in the empire if I stay here. Get our things together. We leave for Rome in a week."

But he wasn't happy in Rome either. After only a year, a friend arranged for a teaching job for him in Milan.

"It's a good move for my career," he explained to Amica. "Alypius is coming, too, so we won't be alone there."

They traveled to Milan and moved into a small house near the public bath.

"You are the new rhetoric teacher?" asked an old neighbor with watery eyes.

"Yes."

"Then you must go to church on Sunday."

"Thank you for the advice, but I don't worship the Christian god."

"Ah, but you teach public speaking, and Bishop Ambrose is the best orator in Milan. Even the most educated go to hear him preach."

Augustine was curious. He decided to go see this famous preacher.

"You're going to church?" Amica asked, raising an eyebrow.

"Only to study the bishop's technique," he insisted.

He hesitated outside the church. "I haven't been to a Christian service since my mother dragged me there when I was teenager," he thought. "And I swore I would never go back." But if there was anything to learn from this orator, it would serve his career, and that was now the most important thing in his life.

He went inside and slipped into a row next to an old woman. She smelled strongly of onions, and he wrinkled his nose in disgust and thought about moving to another seat. But when the bishop rose and began to speak, Augustine forgot all about her.

Ambrose was not a large man, but his deep voice rang out with power and his eyes flashed as he declared, "This is the Word of the Lord!" He preached like it was his last sermon, leaning forward on his toes and shouting. Light from the altar candles glistened on his high forehead.

Augustine was stunned by the preacher's ability. During the whole sermon, he never once thought of Carthage, or Meandus's death, or Old Onion Woman beside him. Only when the bishop concluded his sermon with a flourish and sat down did Augustine remember that he didn't like church.

He left before his seatmate could offer an aromatic hello.

"I've never heard anyone speak that way," he told Alypius after class the next day. "His arguments were well-reasoned and his grammar was perfect. The congregation barely breathed while he was speaking! He held their attention for the entire sermon."

"Are you going back?"

"I have no interest in his subject matter, but just observing this man in action will advance my career."

"Then I'll go with you. You have me curious about Ambrose."

Augustine was surprised to get a visitor one afternoon shortly after he got home from class. "Mother!" he cried when he opened the door. "What are you doing in Milan?"

"Is that any way to greet your mother?" she said, drawing him into a hug. "I've rented a house down the street."

"It's good to see you, Mother, but why are you here?"

Her eyes twinkled. "I heard you've been attending Bishop Ambrose's church. You can't imagine how happy that makes me!"

He frowned. "I only go to learn his technique."

"All that matters right now is that you are going to church. I hope you won't mind if I come with you on Sunday."

He stared at her and laughed. "You're going to do it anyway, aren't you?"

For several months they attended Ambrose's services together. The church wasn't far from their neighborhood, so on Sunday mornings, Augustine met his mother at her house and walked her to and from the service.

On the way home one Sunday, Monica chattered about her recent visits to some of the local martyrs' shrines. "In Thagaste, I used to take baskets of cake and wine to the shrines to honor the dead saints. But here, Bishop Ambrose does not allow the practice. Did you know that?"

He gave her a blank look and adjusted his belt. "Did I know what?"

She laughed at him. "You haven't heard a word I've said."

"I'm sorry," he said. "I was thinking about the bishop's sermon on the Song of Solomon this morning."

"Oh?"

"I just can't get over the way he preaches. It's like he knows my objections to Christianity and every week his goal is to refute them."

She grabbed his arm and stopped. "Do you mean he's convinced you to become a Christian?"

"Not yet," he said with a smile. "You don't think it's that easy, do you?"

She turned to him with her intense black eyes. "My son, it is not easy for any of us to follow Christ."

"You have given up the world, but I'm not ready to do that. I'm dissatisfied with the Manicheans now, but the writings of Plato may contain what I'm looking for."

"You are still running from God."

"Ambrose has sparked my interest, but I'm not going to accept his teachings until I have studied all the options."

"Do what you need to do," said Monica. "I still pray for you every day, as I have since you were a child. I am confident that before I die, you will be a Christian."

On a summer evening, Augustine joined Alypius for dinner at an inn near the marketplace. They were pushing back their empty wooden platters when Alypius said, "I have a confession to make. I went to see the bishop today."

"You did? Why?"

"I had a few questions for him."

"What did he say?"

"Nothing. There was a long line of people there to seek his advice, ask for help getting a job, or have him pray for them. I didn't want to wait. I think he's the busiest man in Milan."

"I know what you mean. I went to see him a few days ago, too."

Alypius leaned across the table. "You didn't tell me that!"

Augustine laughed. "There was nothing to tell. I went to the church after dinner, hoping everyone would have gone home. He was there in his office, but he was reading quietly, and he looked like he needed some time to himself. I didn't want to bother him, so I left."

"What were you going to ask him about? Astrology?"

"No. Firminus has finally convinced me of the folly of astrology. I wanted to talk to the bishop about marriage."

Alypius raised an eyebrow. "He's not married."

"I know. But I wanted to hear what the Bible says about it."

"Why? What are you not telling me?"

Augustine sighed. "My mother thinks I should get married. A wife from an important family would advance my career."

"A wife would distract you from your career," Alypius declared, throwing up his hands. "I thought we were going to build a community for professional thinkers. Your patron has already promised the funds."

"Many good thinkers are married."

Alypius folded his arms across his chest. "What about Amica?"

Frowning, Augustine stared at a smoky lantern on the wall. "You know that by law, I cannot marry her. I can only marry a woman of my own class. And my mother says my life with Amica is a sin and a hindrance to my future."

"Since when do you care what your mother thinks?"

"She's right, Alypius. As long as I am with Amica, the influential people will look down on me. Even if I never marry, I can't live with her anymore. It's killing my career."

"It sounds like you've already made a decision."

Augustine slumped down in his seat. "I have. Amica is going back to her parents in Carthage. She leaves in three days."

"What about Adeodatus?"

"He's staying with me." He buried his face in his hands. "I have to say good-bye to the woman I love, but I will not give up my son."

Alypius paid for their meals and walked his unhappy friend home.

Monica was so glad her son was taking her advice that she offered her own carriage to take Amica to the waiting ship to North Africa. When the horses drew up outside the house, Adeodatus threw his arms around his mother.

"Mother, don't go!" the boy begged.

Augustine watched them in misery. "The boy is almost as tall as his mother," he thought. They were both crying, and he noticed again that they had the same black eyes with a heavy fringe of lashes, now wet with tears. He put a gentle hand on his son's shoulder. "You know she can't stay. But maybe someday you can visit her in Carthage."

Amica hugged her son desperately and turned sad, shining eyes on Augustine. "I will never love another man for as long as I live," she whispered. She wrenched herself away from her sobbing boy and fled to the carriage. Adeodatus ran into the house.

Numb, Augustine stood alone and watched the carriage disappear down the street.

During the following months, he retreated to his life of thought with Alypius. He spent extra time with his students. He missed Amica, and was tortured by his search for truth. He kept going to church with Monica, discussing Ambrose's sermons later with his friends.

One afternoon, Augustine and Alypius were relaxing at a friend's villa. Alypius was stretched out on the floor gazing aimlessly at the mosaic ceiling. Augustine was reading. The quiet afternoon was interrupted by a surprise visit from a friend.

"Ponticianus!" Augustine said, setting aside his book and rising to greet his guest. "What is an important officer of the court doing here?"

Ponticianus grinned. "I heard you were staying here and thought I would drop in and see my old friends. I hope I'm not disturbing you."

"Not at all."

The visitor spotted Augustine's book on the table. "So, what does the great teacher read? A book of law? The work of a great philosopher?"

Augustine handed his friend the book. "The Apostle Paul's letter to the Romans."

Ponticianus looked at him in surprise. "Are you a Christian?"

"Not really."

"What does that mean?"

"It means he's afraid to make the commitment," Alypius said with a laugh. "He just keeps talking about it."

"I've been studying Scripture for several months." Augustine shrugged and sat down on a couch, gesturing for his friends to do the same.

Ponticianus set the book back on the table. "Have either of you heard the story of Saint Antony, the Egyptian monk?"

Alypius looked at Augustine. "I haven't."

"Saint Antony was a successful man, much like the two of you," Ponticianus said, leaning back. "He was from a wealthy family in a small village. When his parents died, he received a large inheritance and planned to live a life of comfort. But when he heard the gospel preached at church and read Christ's command to the rich young ruler to forsake all and follow him, he was moved to give up his luxury. He dedicated his life to serving Christ and his church."

"He wasn't the first to give away his possessions for an ideal," Augustine said.

"No," agreed Ponticianus. "But his life became a great inspiration to many others. Bishop Athanasius of Alexandria respected him so much that he wrote a book about his life. Two friends of mine, both high-ranking civil servants and friends of the emperor himself, were so inspired by the story that they also gave up their influential positions to follow Christ. They realized that their lives of luxury were a barrier to loving Christ."

Augustine was troubled by the conversation. He stared uneasily at the paintings of warriors and hunters on the walls. "They might as well be paintings of my own sin, displayed for all the world to see," he thought.

When Ponticianus left, he stood up in agitation. "What is wrong with us, Alypius? People without all our knowledge and education are capturing heaven, but we, with all our advantages, are missing the truth. Are we ashamed to follow Christ or are we ashamed to be counted with those who are less sophisticated?"

Alypius stared at him, his brow furrowed in concentration.

Augustine picked up the book and pressed it between the palms of his hands. "After thirty-two years, what am I waiting for? Am I foolish enough to trust in my own abilities, rather than in God's grace?"

He ran out to the garden and dropped the book on a table. Alypius followed him in silence, stopping at a polite distance.

Augustine threw himself under a fig tree and began to weep, face down in the dirt. "I keep saying, tomorrow. Why should I wait to end a sinful life tomorrow?" he asked himself. "Why not today?"

He was close enough to the garden wall that he could hear children playing on the other side. Their laughter came to him as he lay under the tree. The sound was calming. "Pick up and read," one of them said. He sat up suddenly and listened, feeling the breeze on his tear-dampened face. "Pick up and read, pick up and read," they chanted. "What child's game is this?" he wondered. "Read what? The book of Romans?"

He jumped to his feet and ran back to the table, snatching up the book. Opening it, his eyes fell on the words of Romans 13:13: "Not in riots and drunkenness, not in partying and indecencies, not in strife and rivalry, but put on the Lord Jesus Christ and make no provision for the flesh in its lusts."

Put on the Lord Jesus Christ. "God, you have made us for yourself and our hearts are restless until they rest in you!" he realized. "This is the answer, Alypius," he said quietly. "I have searched for truth all my life, and it was here, in the Scriptures, all the time."

Alypius took the book from him and read, and looked up at his friend with a smile. "This is freedom from our searching."

"Yes. Our quest is over, Alypius. I must tell my mother."

They rushed to find Monica.

The two young men put their education to work for the church. After being baptized and ordained, Alypius returned home as the bishop of Thagaste. Augustine became the bishop of Hippo, also in North Africa, and eventually was known as the greatest theologian since the Apostle Paul. He wrote many books, including The City of God *and the famous story of his conversion, known as* The Confessions. *He died in 430.*

John Chrysostom: Vanity of Vanities

397 AD. ANTIOCH.

DIM LAMPS LIT the gate near the martyr's shrine just outside of the city. A man with a cloak pulled up around his ears glanced left and right, as a cloaked man might be expected to do. As he peered into the thick darkness, he heard a hurried hoofbeat, and a carriage suddenly lurched to a halt at the gate. He saw a flash of steel as armed guards leaped off the carriage and seized him by the arms.

"What is this?" he demanded, as he was forced into the carriage. "Release me!"

The guards shoved him onto a seat next to a shrouded figure. With the snarling neighs of the horses, the carriage plunged back into the darkness and away from the city.

"John Chrysostom," greeted a familiar voice. "How is our famous presbyter these days?"

"Governor Asterius?" John peered through the darkness at the shadowy figure. "You're the one who sent me the mysterious message to meet at the shrine? What is all this about?"

The figure leaned across the seat and uncovered a lantern, releasing a soft light inside the coach. From inside his cloak he pulled a letter and handed it to John. "You are an important preacher, Golden Mouth." His heavy mustache could not conceal a teasing grin. "The emperor ordered you to be removed as quietly as possible."

"Removed! Removed to where?"

"He's sending you to Constantinople. Bishop Nektarius is dead. Congratulations, Golden Mouth, you are the new bishop of one of the most important cities in the empire!"

"Bishop of Constantinople! But why didn't he just tell me to go? Why am I being taken like this?"

Asterius shook his head. "I really did expect you to be more excited about this promotion! You've spent too many years as a monk, learning how to be unpleasant."

John did look unpleasant as he scowled. The shadows in the carriage exaggerated his piercing eyes, prominent nose, and hollow cheeks. A difficult life had taken a toll on his thin frame.

"Ten years ago, the emperor imposed a tax on Antioch and the city rioted," said Asterius. "He was grateful for the way you calmed the people with your fancy preaching. Now his son Arcadius wants to reward you, and Constantinople needs a new bishop. It's an obvious decision."

"Why kidnap me?"

"Given your popularity, he didn't want to risk another riot when he announced you were leaving, so he's sending you in secret. Only Bishop Flavian was told about the plan."

It was a long journey to Constantinople. After two weeks of travel, the carriage pulled up to a beautiful new building called Holy Sophia Church. In the heart of the city, near the Senate and the palace, it was John's new home. At the church door he was met by a thin, smiling woman with graying hair pinned back from her face. She was surrounded by several clergy in white tunics.

"Welcome, Bishop John," she said. "I am Olympias, the senior deaconess of Sophia. I will be responsible for your meals and laundry. We will be working closely together."

"It's a pleasure to meet you," said John. "Bishop Flavian has spoken of your disciplined life. He says you are a generous woman."

"You are very kind. May we show you around?"

"Please do."

He introduced himself to the presbyters and they went inside.

Beautiful windows filled the church with light. Pillars soared up to the high ceiling, decorated with colorful murals. Strolling through the vast sanctuary Olympias and the clergy updated John on life at Sophia.

"I'm sure Flavian has told you a great deal about the politics of Constantinople," said Olympias. "Emperor Arcadius and Empress Eudoxia consider themselves dedicated Christians. They are part of your new congregation. So is Eutropius, the emperor's chamberlain and one of the few people that have his ear. We understand that he is the one who recommended you for this position."

John's eyes were drawn to the ornate panels around the altar. "I've heard of Eutropius," he replied, turning back to her. "He climbed from slavery to one of the highest positions in the empire."

"Yes, and he was almost solely responsible for arranging the emperor's marriage." She leaned away from the clergy and whispered, "He is also unpredictable, so be careful."

Vincent, one of the presbyters, cleared his throat. "Theophilus, Bishop of Alexandria, will preside over your installation."

"The governor warned me that Theophilus might oppose me."

"Evidently Theophilus insisted on his own nominee for your position," said Olympias. "An eighty-year-old presbyter named Isidore."

"We all expected the emperor to appoint Isidore," said Vincent. "But rumor has it that Eutropius blackmailed Theophilus, forcing him to back down, and the emperor chose you instead."

"Welcome to Constantinople," said Olympias with a chuckle. She headed swiftly down the corridor.

"Lord, grant me the grace to serve you here," he prayed as he went after her.

John stepped confidently into his new position. The powerful preaching that had earned him his nickname quickly caught the attention of Constantinople. As his congregation grew, so did his challenges.

One afternoon, Sarapion, John's strong-willed archdeacon, came to his office. A tall man with broad shoulders and a piercing gaze, Sarapion was opinionated. Not everyone liked him. But John ordained him as a deacon because he was a godly man and had a reputation for getting things done.

"How is our investigation going?" asked John, standing to welcome his colleague.

"We continue to find clergy who are undisciplined, indulgent, and immoral." The deacon scanned the books on John's shelves with interest. "I hear you are having trouble with the monk named Isaac."

"Yes," said John with a deep sigh. "A monk is supposed to live a life separate from the world and its temptations. He vows to converse only with God and live in discipline. But the monks here live lavishly. They're undisciplined, even to the point of protests in the streets!"

"I've found similar problems with the clergy. I believe there are at least two deacons who are guilty of murder."

"Murder!"

"I'm afraid so. The morals of the clergy are a disgrace. They enjoy more pleasures than Satan himself!"

"So it appears."

"That is why God brought you here," said Sarapion with a smile. "He is using you to end the corruption."

"I'm doing my best. But if these problems weren't enough——." John lowered his voice and glanced at the door. "Eutropius seems to think that I owe him something. I'm grateful for his recommendation to this post, but he keeps using it to ask for favors. So far, I've been able to avoid confrontation, but I don't know how long that will last."

"Eutropius doesn't take no for an answer. Many of his enemies are rotting in prison, or have simply disappeared." He turned to leave. "Be careful, Bishop."

John walked Sarapion to the door. "Our biggest problems are right here at the church. We need to do something about the clergy."

"Agreed," said Sarapion with a nod. "But many good bishops have found themselves at odds with Eutropius. Watch yourself."

John asked God for direction. Then he set out to reform the church of Constantinople the way he knew best—by preaching. With his golden mouth, he encouraged his congregation to become missionaries to the Gothic people who had settled in the city. He argued for the removal of pagan altars. The people listened like they had in Antioch. Even when he preached against sports and entertainment on Sunday, his congregation begged him for more sermons. Emperor Arcadius and his right-hand man Eutropius did not like all of John's reforms, but they cooperated—for a while.

On a weekday morning, John headed out of Sophia. He enjoyed taking walks through the city, praying, and planning his next sermon. As he stepped out into the morning air, he glanced up just as a man stumbled into him.

"Can I help you?" John asked.

The man looked over his shoulder and mumbled an apology.

Running into the sanctuary, he wrapped his arms around the altar. As John followed him, he heard the man saying, "Lord, help me! Lord, help me!"

The bishop knelt beside him. "Are you in trouble, brother? How can I help you?"

"They're coming for me," the man whimpered. "They want to arrest me, but I'm innocent!"

John looked up as two soldiers appeared at the open church door. They didn't enter, but nodded respectfully at John. "Good morning, Bishop," one called. "We've come for the man at the altar."

"He says he didn't do anything," John replied.

"Eutropius ordered his immediate arrest."

"Eutropius knows the rules," John said, laying a hand on the frightened man's shoulder. "If anyone seeks asylum in a church, it is granted. You cannot take him away unless he leaves the building."

The soldiers hesitated.

"Tell Eutropius that this man is safe in my custody."

They left.

Olympias came from around the corner where she had been watching and gave the man a friendly smile. "Come with me," she said. "You can stay with the others." As she passed John, she whispered, "If Eutropius continues to treat people this way, we'll run out of room at the church!"

"Then we'll have a full service on Sunday!" said John. "I'll meet with Eutropius and see if I can work all this out."

Later that day John received word that Eutropius wanted to see him. He went to the palace at the appointed time, and was quietly escorted through the halls to Eutropius's chambers.

"Wait here," said the servant.

From where he stood outside the door, John could hear a loud conversation.

"Sir, I'm afraid Gainas has the upper hand." The voice had a soldier's discipline.

"That's ridiculous!" came the angry response. John recognized the arrogant voice of Eutropius. "Gainas is a general under Emperor Arcadius, and therefore under me."

The soldier replied with a respectful but serious tone. "We discovered that he and his barbarian allies, led by Tribigild, were secretly plotting against you. They threatened to have you removed from the emperor's service."

"Arcadius won't take him seriously."

"Sir, my sources say that Gainas may even have a private army to take you by force if necessary."

"I can handle Gainas," Eutropius said confidently. "I didn't make it to this position without being one step ahead of the others."

"Yes, sir. But you should also know that one of the empress's ladies told me Eudoxia is supporting Gainas."

John was startled by the sound of pottery breaking. He took a step away from the curtained doorway and glanced around the hall.

"I arranged Arcadius's marriage to Eudoxia," said Eutropius, his voice low and threatening. "I brought her into this kingdom. I can have her banished! Make sure your men know that I am in charge here."

"Yes, sir. We will not fail you."

"Send John in!"

The curtain was swept back, and the soldier marched out without a glance at John. The bishop went in. He expected Eutropius to be fuming, but instead he seemed calm.

"Johhhnnnn," drawled Eutropius, as if he hadn't seen an old friend in a long time. "Come in, and ignore the mess. I had a little accident with the water basin." The remains of the basin were scattered across the floor.

"Thank you for the invitation," said John. "I was hoping to visit you this week."

"Then my timing is good. We need to talk about the church's practice of granting asylum." The smile dropped from his face.

"I see. What is the problem?"

"I think the problem is obvious. You welcome criminals into your church, and turn away my soldiers."

"Asylum is recognized by the empire," reminded John.

"It was recognized," corrected Eutropius with a smirk. "But today, with my influence, legislation was passed that makes it illegal. The condemned can no longer escape their punishment by running to the church."

"But many people claim to be falsely accused. What about the innocent?"

"They are lying, of course."

John glared at him, his jaw tightening. "You are fighting the authority of the church, Eutropius. You don't want to do this."

"I have, and I will enforce it," said Eutropius. "I expect you to do so as well. After all, a bishop should never help criminals."

"I can't go along with this."

"Surely you haven't forgotten how I convinced Theophilus to end his campaign for Isidore and support your appointment instead?"

"I never asked you to do that," insisted John. "And I'm sure you got something in return, whatever it was."

Eutropius turned and walked to a window, motioning to a guard at the door. "Thank you for coming so late this evening, Bishop."

John left. Later, he approached the emperor in complaint, but the emperor refused to listen.

It was a few weeks later, on a Saturday night, that John was shaken from his prayers by the clank of armor in the church.

"Soldiers usually leave their armor and weapons at the door," he thought. "They must be chasing someone seeking asylum." John walked quickly through the halls of Sophia to intercept the soldiers.

"Where is he?" said one of the soldiers as John approached. "We don't want to cause trouble in the church, but he must come with us now!"

John blocked the corridor, his hands on his hips. "No one shall violate this sanctuary," he said in a quiet, deliberate tone. "The church is the bride of Christ, and I am entrusted with her honor. You will have to arrest me first."

"Please, Bishop, you must hand over Eutropius," the soldier insisted.

"Eutropius? The emperor's chamberlain?"

He heard angry voices out in the courtyard. "Give us Eutropius! Execute Eutropius!"

"What's going on here?" John demanded.

A crash interrupted his question. He ran to the door and saw a crowd throwing rocks at a fallen statue of the chamberlain.

"Can't this city go one day without a riot?" complained a soldier. "Come on, we'd better handle this. We'll come back for the criminal."

As they filed past, a soldier stopped at John's side. The bishop recognized him as a member of the church. "It is said," whispered the soldier, "that the empress heard Eutropius threaten to send her away. She went to Emperor Arcadius in tears, holding their two young daughters, and told him of the plot. Now Arcadius wants Eutropius's head."

"He will have to wait a long time," John insisted, "because I will not let you take anyone, even Eutropius."

The soldiers waited respectfully outside the church all night. Word that Eutropius had sought asylum in the church drew a huge crowd to the service the next morning. When Sophia's doors were opened, crowds of citizens and soldiers poured into the sanctuary. The emperor was the most eager of all, taking his usual seat at the front. He was ready to demand that Eutropius be brought forward, but he held back his impatience, curious to see how the bishop would handle the situation.

When the veil that covered the altar was removed, the congregation gasped in surprise. Eutropius clung to the altar with white knuckles, exhausted from his sleepless night. John came up the aisle and took his place next to the altar. With all eyes focused on Eutropius, he began his morning sermon. "Vanity of vanities!" cried John. "All is vanity! Thus says the preacher in the book of Ecclesiastes."

He scanned the congregation, his gaze resting on the emperor.

Arcadius, dressed in his finest royal robes, watched him quietly.

"It is always wise to remember this, but especially now. Have I not repeatedly preached to you that wealth, money, fame, and power are fleeting? But you would not believe me. Now we see from experience that it is true. The life that craves the pleasures of this world is empty of God!"

The sanctuary was silent.

"I don't say this to make light of Eutropius's misfortune," John continued, "but so you will be more compassionate to the man who once did you wrong. We should thank God that he has given Eutropius time to repent from his sins. Doesn't the Lord teach us that he will forgive us as we forgive others? Eutropius has hurt you, but we are to be merciful, and ask God to show mercy on him, as God has shown mercy on us."

The eyes of the congregation turned from the frightened man at the altar to the splendidly dressed emperor. Arcadius shifted, aware that he was caught in a public object lesson. He looked at John, then at Eutropius, and then at the congregation. Rising, he walked toward the altar. The worshipers didn't dare move, wondering if the emperor would kill Eutropius right there in the church.

"Such a brave man reduced to rubble," said Arcadius, waving a hand at the altar as he turned to face the congregation. "Eutropius has done many things, but Bishop John is right. We should show mercy on him. We should behave better than he would."

John placed a gentle hand on Eutropius's trembling shoulder.

"No one shall touch a hair on his head," Arcadius continued. "He will be punished for his crimes, but not with his life. He will be exiled far from here. His property will be seized and his titles removed. But his life will be spared."

The people cheered the emperor's merciful actions as soldiers stepped forward to safely escort Eutropius outside. When the sun set that night, the right of asylum had been restored and John's foe had been replaced by a new chamberlain named Aurelianus. John thanked God for his intervention.

A few months later Olympias knocked at John's office door with a kitchen tray. "Are you ready for your meal?"

"I've been so intent on finishing this sermon, I didn't realize how late it is. Thank you."

She set the plate of bread in front of him. "Have you heard about Eutropius?"

"Has he returned to Constantinople?" He lifted a water jug from the tray and took a long swig.

"Not exactly."

He looked at her worried eyes and frowned. "What's happened?"

She sat on a stool and leaned her elbows on his desk. "The new chamberlain, Aurelianus, and General Gainas accused Eutropius of new charges. Some say falsely accused. But Eudoxia supported their claims."

"What are they claiming as his crime?"

"High treason. They seized him at Cyprus and had him beheaded."

They sat in silence for a moment. Then John said quietly, "These are dangerous people in our congregation."

"Yes," she agreed.

"But God is more powerful," he said suddenly with confidence. "And he has a lot of work for us to do in this big city."

"Well, my work right now is to make sure God's Golden Mouth eats his dinner." She grinned and pushed the plate toward him.

He stood. "Let's see if Sarapion wants to join us. I hear he keeps a supply of delicious pastries to deny himself the indulgence."

"Then by all means, let's help him in that pursuit!" They laughed and headed for the deacon's office.

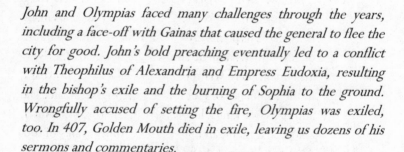

John and Olympias faced many challenges through the years, including a face-off with Gainas that caused the general to flee the city for good. John's bold preaching eventually led to a conflict with Theophilus of Alexandria and Empress Eudoxia, resulting in the bishop's exile and the burning of Sophia to the ground. Wrongfully accused of setting the fire, Olympias was exiled, too. In 407, Golden Mouth died in exile, leaving us dozens of his sermons and commentaries.

HOW DID WE GET THE BIBLE?

THE NAME BIBLE comes from the Greek word for "books." It first referred to the sheets or rolls made from papyrus plants used to make books. The 39 books of the Old Testament and the 27 books of the New Testament were written over a period of 1,400 years, in the languages of Hebrew, Greek, and Aramaic. The authors were kings, legislators, shepherds, fishermen, a doctor, a rabbi, and people from other walks of life, who lived in the lands of Israel, Italy, Greece, and Asia Minor (now known as Turkey). The original hand-written pages or *manuscripts* of the Bible no longer exist. In those days long before copy machines, faithful scribes copied the originals by hand to share the books with other Christians. These copyists preserved for us the reliable texts we use today.

During the Old Testament period, books were kept in the temple and used for worship. As the number of these books grew, they were collected and categorized into groups of Law, Prophets, and Writings. Some of the books we have today, like Ezra and

Nehemiah, were originally one book. The collection of books recognized today as the Old Testament was fixed somewhere around the year 250 BC, or 250 years before Jesus was born. At this time, the Old Testament, written mostly in Hebrew, was translated into Greek, the common language of the day. Often these books were combined with other books known as the *Apocrypha*, or "hidden things." These extra books of the Apocrypha are not considered to have the same authority as the Old Testament.

While the Old Testament was being collected in its current form, the New Testament was being written. The New Testament is made up of the four Gospels that tell the story of Jesus' birth and death, the letters of the Apostle Paul, and letters by some of the other apostles. When Jesus rose from the dead and ascended into heaven, he sent his Holy Spirit to inspire his disciples to write the New Testament books. The Bible says that the Holy Spirit taught the disciples "all things" and reminded them of everything Jesus had taught them while he was on earth (John 16:12-13). They wrote these letters to Christians in various cities, encouraging them to live godly lives and correcting errors in their beliefs. As the New Testament writers wrote, God confirmed their authority as apostles of Jesus by giving them the power to perform miracles. The early Christians who received these letters from the apostles considered the letters to have the same divine authority as the Old Testament, and copied them to send to other Christians.

But like the Apocrypha of the Old Testament, there were other books being written at the time of the New Testament, and sometime these books were included with the writings of Paul. God gave the early Christians the job of recognizing which of these books belonged to the *canon* of Scripture. The word canon means "reed," a sturdy river plant that was used as a measuring stick. We call the Bible the canon because it is God's authoritative rule for our lives.

The Christian teachers of the first few centuries, or *church fathers*, including Irenaeus, Hippolytus, Tertullian, Origen, and Eusebius, examined all the books and made lists of the ones they considered authentic and the ones they considered apocryphal. One of the most valuable lists comes from Athanasius, the bishop of Alexandria. As was the custom of bishops in his day, Athanasius wrote letters to the church on Easter. In his famous Easter letter of the year 367 AD, he confirms the 39 Old Testament books and the 27 New Testament books we have today. A few books were disputed over the years, but gradually the church fathers developed a final list of the biblical books.

In 245, after 15 years of work, Origen published his Hexapla, providing six versions of the Old Testament in side-by-side columns, including the original Hebrew text and a Greek translation. About 150 years later, Jerome used this book to make a fresh translation of the Old Testament from Hebrew to Latin, the common language in the western part of the empire. The *Vulgate* (meaning "common") became the standard version of the Old Testament until well into the medieval period.

Today, the Bible has been translated into almost every language of the world, and more copies have been printed of the Bible than any other book. When you open your copy of the Bible, thank God for the prophets and apostles he used to write his Word and for the church fathers he used to put it together. Through the faithfulness of these men, God preserved the story of his salvation for you to love and study.

JEROME: LOVE THE HOLY SCRIPTURES, AND WISDOM WILL LOVE YOU

403 AD. BETHLEHEM, A QUIET VILLAGE IN PALESTINE.

SCOWLING, JEROME HUNCHED over the table and squinted at the page of squiggles. "These tiny letters are hard enough to read without my bad eyes," he grumbled.

"Yes, sir, but you're almost finished," replied the young man working at his side. "Soon you will have translated the entire Old Testament from Hebrew into Latin."

"I know what an achievement it is!" Jerome snapped. "I'm the scholar here, remember?"

The scribe put down his quill and stared at the floor. "Yes, sir."

"I'm going out," Jerome said, snatching up his walking stick. "Finish copying that book by Origen while I'm gone." He stomped out the door and winced in the glare of the low-hanging afternoon sun. The long hours he spent every day in his office translating the Bible and writing essays irritated his already weak eyes.

Frowning, he shook his head. "You lost your temper again, old man," he thought. "This work is so important, but some days the

179

burden is too much for my patience."

Turning his back to the sun, he gazed across the broad limestone ridge. To the southeast lay the little village of Bethlehem, surrounded by corn fields and pastures, and beyond that, the red pillars of the Church of the Nativity. Closer to him, a wide strip of garden separated two building clusters. On this side was the monastery he supervised. On the other side, along the main road, was the hospital and women's monastery managed by his friend Paula.

He began to descend the hillside. Walking past a row of huts that served as sleeping quarters for the monks, his thoughts turned to how this community had begun.

"Paula really should get the credit," he thought. "She does most of the work around here."

They had met in Rome when he was working as the bishop's assistant, right after he had started this translation project. Rome was the heart of politics and commerce. Built on seven hills on the banks of the Tiber River, the city was dotted with churches, pagan temples, and public baths. People from the farthest corners of the empire cheered in their native dialects at chariot races and debated philosophy in the forum.

But Jerome had no time, and no interest, for these distractions. Bishop Damasus gave him a small apartment and kept him busy writing essays and letters for the church. It was the elderly Damasus who first suggested he revise the popular Latin version of the Bible. That had been over twenty years ago.

"The Old Testament was written in Hebrew," Damasus had said in his rough, wobbly voice, "but even before Jesus was born, Greek had become the standard language. The translators of our Latin Bible based their version on the Greek translation, instead of on the original Hebrew. You're the first Christian I know of to learn Hebrew. You should prepare a new, more accurate translation for the Latin-speaking church."

The project seemed like a challenge for someone with his education and academic abilities. So he accepted the task. Starting with the Gospels, he began to re-translate books of the Old and New Testaments. Christians in Rome started to notice the bishop's assistant.

One day he was summoned to the home of Marcella, a widow and a friend of Damasus. The address was in a rich neighborhood on the Aventine, the most southern of the seven hills. When a slave girl answered his knock, he followed her into a vast, empty room. Three walls were covered with cheerful murals of fruit and flowers.

"This way," she said.

They crossed to the far side of the room, which opened onto a covered courtyard. Between yellow columns stood life-size statues of young women with water jars. To Jerome's right and left, the courtyard opened onto numerous smaller rooms and stairways. Straight ahead, open to the sky, the courtyard led to a garden of trees and flowering shrubs. In the center, reclining on low couches, a group of women were gathered around a fountain. One of the women rose as he entered the garden.

"Thank you for coming," she said, welcoming him with a regal nod. A shaft of afternoon sun lit up her silver-streaked hair, tucked into a simple knot. Jerome noticed immediately that she was beautiful, but dressed in a plain, loose garment, with a linen belt tied high around her waist. "There's something different about her," he thought. "These rich Roman women are usually fond of their elaborate hairstyles and expensive clothes."

"I'm Marcella," she said, gesturing to the other women in the circle, "and this is my mother Albina, my friend Lea, Paula, and Paula's daughters Blesilla and Eustochium." They were all dressed in the same simple fashion as Marcella.

"We are honored to meet you, sir," said Paula. "Won't you sit down?"

"Thank you." He leaned back on a couch under a shade tree.

"I'm sure you're wondering why I asked you to come," Marcella said as she returned to her seat. "We all live here, worshiping God and studying the Bible together. But we have many questions about the Scriptures, and Damasus says you are the man to answer them. Will you teach us?"

"What do you want to know?"

Marcella leaned forward eagerly. "The book of Exodus speaks of an *ephod*. What is that?"

"It's a garment worn by Jewish priests."

"Ah," she nodded. "Many of the Psalms use the word *selah*. What does it mean?"

"Scholars aren't sure," Jerome said, shrugging. "It's probably a musical term since the Psalms were written to be sung."

"Damasus was right about you," Marcella said. "You can teach us a lot about the Bible."

"Your flattery is kind," Jerome said, rising. "But I am very busy with an important translation project. Surely Damasus or one of the local presbyters can answer your questions."

"We want to learn Hebrew and Greek." The statement was matter of fact. It came from Paula, who had jumped to her feet.

Jerome squinted at her and scowled. "I understand why you want to learn Greek. Educated people read Greek. But I'm the only Christian who knows Hebrew."

Paula smiled and lifted her chin triumphantly. "That's why you are the only one who can teach us."

"She has a bright, earnest face," Jerome decided. He looked back at Marcella, who was watching him closely. "This is a curious group of women."

"All right, I'll take you on as students," he agreed. "But if you're not devoted to your studies, I'm not going to waste my valuable time."

Marcella raised a delicate eyebrow and looked him straight in the eye. "You won't find more devoted students in a monastery," she promised.

Jerome was a good teacher, and the women learned easily. They weren't intimidated by him like some of the men he worked with. He began to look forward to the lessons and developed friendships with his pupils.

After a lesson one day, Jerome and Paula strolled through Marcella's courtyard garden.

"Where did you learn Hebrew?" Paula asked.

"It's a long story. My parents sent me to the best schools. I was an ambitious student, but I was also distracted by worldly desires. I thought if I isolated myself from other people and gave up comfort, I could discipline myself. So I became a hermit in the Syrian desert. I lived in a cave, slept on the hard ground, and wore animal hair."

"That must have been lonely!"

"Well, it would have been without my scribes."

"You had scribes in the desert? What did you need scribes for?"

"They were copying my books."

Paula threw her head back and laughed. "You lived in a cave and wore scraps of animal hide, but you had books with you?"

He shrugged and grinned. "I could give up my bed, but I just couldn't give up my library."

"For a scholar like you, I'm sure your library is your most precious possession." She paused in a corner of the garden near a fountain and settled on a low stone wall. "But how did you learn Hebrew?"

"One of the other hermits that lived in a nearby cave was a Jew who had converted to Christianity. I've always been good at languages, and I wanted to be able to read the Old Testament in the language it was written in, so I convinced him to become my tutor."

"And now you're teaching us," Paula said. "Thank God you had room in your cave for your books, your scribes, and your Jewish neighbor! What a poor, lonely hermit you were!"

Jerome glared at her through narrow eyes. "It was a hard life," he said defensively. "I would have continued there, but I realized my talents were being wasted in that cave."

"There is more than one way to serve God," Paula said gently. "Some are meant to live as hermits, but some are meant to be where they can teach others."

Jerome's cynical features softened. "You're right, of course. After my desert experience, I went to Constantinople and studied Scripture with Gregory of Nazianzus. I learned a lot from his teaching."

"Another great privilege! You've had such an exciting life."

"I suppose." Absently, he stuck his hand in the fountain and redirected the water with his palm. Ripples distorted the seashells and multicolored tiles that studded the bottom of the pool.

"I'm sorry," he said, shaking the water off his hand. "I've been talking about myself the whole time. It's my turn to ask about you."

"What about me?"

"I can see that you and Marcella are rich, yet you both choose to live simply instead of flaunting your wealth."

"God has generously provided for us," Paula replied, running her fingertips over the rough fabric that covered her knees. "Marcella's a much stronger woman than I, and so intelligent, as you have noticed. When her husband died twenty-five years ago, she could have remarried anyone or invested her money in business. But she read a book about Antony by Bishop Athanasius, and admired the discipline of those desert monks. She was determined to live as they did and started a Bible-reading group here in her villa."

"Is that how you met?"

"Yes. Like most wealthy women, I used to put my energy into getting my hair curled and buying new clothes. Almost every day I threw a big party and got drunk with my friends." She sighed with obvious regret. "When my husband died a few years ago, I decided to devote my attention to God instead of a new man. I heard about Marcella's Bible study through some friends who were gossiping about how odd and disgraceful she had become."

Jerome struck at the wall with his sandal. "How dare those vipers look down on her! She has chosen a holier life."

"If you had been here to defend her, I'm sure they wouldn't have had the nerve!" She gave him a friendly smile and plucked a leaf from a potted herb at her elbow. "Her guidance is just what I have needed. She is helping me raise my daughters to know that Bible study and prayer are much more valuable than expensive jewelry and perfume. We've given up everything that might distract us from living for God."

He tilted his head and looked at her approvingly. "We have a lot in common then," he said. "Thank you for the conversation. It's time I got back to my work."

"And I must round up my daughters for evening prayers."

"You are a wise woman, Paula," he said as he left. "Others should follow your example."

He went back to his apartment, thoughtful of Paula's story. Within days, he published a sharp essay criticizing the lavish lifestyles of church members. Roman society frowned as they discussed his pamphlets over their nightly feasts.

"You are not making friends, Jerome," Damasus warned him. "Must you always speak your mind?"

"But I'm right!" Jerome insisted. "These Christians are making wealth and popularity their god, and someone must denounce their actions."

The bishop laid a wrinkled hand on his assistant's shoulder. "You are so sure of yourself," he said, shaking his white head. "I support your goal, but perhaps you should change your tactics. A lot of people are demanding that I dismiss you, Jerome. My health is failing. I'll soon be gone, and I'm afraid you will be on your own."

Damasus did what he could to defend his assistant against the rising tide of disapproval. But he was feeble, and Jerome had offended some powerful people. When the bishop died and a successor was appointed, Jerome was deliberately overlooked. It wasn't long before Siricius, the new bishop, called for Jerome's resignation and asked him to leave Rome.

Jerome went straight to Marcella's house and confided in his friends. "What have I done to deserve this treatment?" he complained. "Have I ever gone too far?"

"You always go too far!" Marcella said with a laugh.

He thrust his chin high. "I did what I could, but obviously the people of Rome are not interested in God's ways. It is time to move on."

Marcella and Paula glanced at each other, shaking their heads.

"You are a proud and stubborn man, Jerome," Marcella said, "but I believe God is using you to correct his people."

"Where will you go?" asked Paula.

"I think to Palestine, where Jesus lived."

"I've always wanted to visit Bethlehem!" Paula exclaimed. "And you are going to need a new sponsor for your translation work. Maybe I could meet you there. We could tour all the biblical sites together and you can continue to teach me Hebrew."

Jerome laughed at her enthusiasm. "I'd be grateful for your company, my devoted friend."

He said good-bye and boarded a ship to begin his journey to

Palestine. As the ship pulled out of the harbor, he spat over the stern. "Good riddance," he thought. "I'll never return to that pagan city again."

Paula spent several weeks making arrangements for their journey, and then set sail with her daughter Eustochium and several friends. They soon met up with Jerome and began a year-long tour of the land where Jesus had walked four hundred years earlier.

They visited dozens of cities in Palestine, but their favorite was Bethlehem. It was barely a town, small and quiet with few distractions. A church had been built over the cave where rumors said Jesus was born. They stood in the chamber beneath the church for hours, gazing at the silver vessel that had long ago replaced the real manger. In that little village, so near the place where the baby Jesus had taken his first breath, the story of the Gospels seemed to come alive. They couldn't leave.

"What an ideal place this would be to concentrate on translating," Jerome said.

"It's also perfect for teaching young men and women how to devote themselves to God," Paula replied.

"Well, why not?" suggested Jerome. "You can afford to build something here. Why not found a monastery for women and start teaching Hebrew yourself? You've become rather good at reciting the Old Testament."

"Jerome, was that a compliment?" she said with a delighted smile. "I will never need another encouraging word!"

He glared at her. "I'm serious."

"I think it's a wonderful idea!"

So they had built the twin monasteries, not far from the Church of the Nativity, starting with just a handful of pupils. Now there were dozens of students studying the Bible, learning Greek and Hebrew, and spending their days praying and herding sheep.

"I must be getting old to dwell so much on the past these days," he thought.

A rider approached from the road on horseback, and Jerome stepped up his pace to meet him.

"Vincentius! How good to see you!" He offered a hand to the tall man as he swung down from the horse's back.

"How goes the translation?"

"No one appreciates my work, as usual."

Vincentius grinned. "Of course not. Well, perhaps the winds of scholarship have changed. I have quite a bundle of letters for you." He untied a leather pack and handed it to Jerome.

"More letters to answer," Jerome grumbled, glancing through the stack. "We have a pile ready for you to take with you. But first, some Bethlehem hospitality, eh?" He waved to a blond-haired monk crossing a corn field. "Get our weary visitor some refreshment."

Vincentius went off to the kitchen with the monk. Jerome threw the sack over his shoulder and headed toward the small hospital. Paula came out the door just as he reached it.

"Is that Vincentius with the mail?" she asked eagerly.

"Yes, and there's a whole pile here for you," he said, thrusting the bundle into her weathered hands and taking a seat on a rock.

"A letter from Marcella!" she cried. "And a copy of Bishop Ambrose's commentary on Luke. I asked her to send it."

"Humpf," he mumbled.

"You don't approve?"

"It's nothing others haven't already said. Ambrose is an ugly crow, decked out in feathers stolen from other birds."

"Oh, Jerome, don't speak ill of the dead. And don't be ridiculous." She caressed the parchment volume with interest. "These new bound books are so much more convenient than scrolls, don't you think? Is that another letter from Augustine of Hippo?"

Jerome threw the packet on the grass. "He's complaining that

I haven't written back to him. He even sent copies of his previous letters 'in case I never got them,' he says. He's just a young upstart badgering an old monk to make a name for himself."

"Isn't he in his fifties?"

"Like I said, a young upstart."

"Maybe if you wrote him back he would stop badgering you, as you call it."

"I don't have time to deal with his petty criticisms of my work. I have to finish this translation before I'm dead."

"And how is the translation coming today?"

"Not nearly fast enough. There are so many manuscripts to compare, and my eyesight is slowing me down."

"You must persevere. No one can do it as well as you."

He folded his hands over his walking stick and looked across the pasture. "The critics don't like the sections of it I've already published," he said. "They prefer the old Latin version better just because they memorized it as children, and they don't care if it is more accurate to translate directly from Hebrew."

"People are just suspicious of Hebrew because they can't read it," Paula reminded him firmly.

"And that is why this work is important. The church cannot grow in God's wisdom without his word. Love the holy Scriptures, and wisdom will love you."

"Because you love it, I know your version is going to become the standard. History will remember you for this."

Jerome gave her a rare smile. "You must have my share of patience as well as your own, Paula. I certainly don't have any, and it would take a double dose to be my friend for all these years."

"Well, you're certainly not an easy man to get along with!" she said, smiling back. "You're as opinionated, proud, and rude as you were when I first met you! But you're as hard on yourself as you are on others. I know that you're just very serious about the truth."

"I suppose I'm too serious."

"You've been called to a difficult, lonely life, Jerome."

"I'll never be lonely as long as you are my friend, Paula." He stood. "I must get back to this translation."

He left her at the hospital reading the letter from Marcella and climbed back up the hill. His faithful scribe was concentrating on the manuscript he was copying and didn't hear him come in. Jerome cleared his throat.

The young man looked up and shifted nervously.

"Excellent work," Jerome said, peering over his shoulder. "Why don't we put that aside for later and get back to this translation project? Someone recently reminded me that we're almost finished."

The monk grinned. "Yes, sir. Here is where we left off."

Jerome took the Hebrew scroll and sighed. "God give me the patience to finish this project," he said.

"Amen!" said the scribe.

Paula died in 404, a year before Jerome published the final instalment of his new translation, which became known as the Vulgate. Marcella was killed in 410 when the Goth king Alaric I invaded Rome. Ten years later, the translator died of old age at his monastery in Bethlehem.

Patrick: Come walk among us

405 AD. BRITAIN, NORTHWESTERN OUTSKIRTS OF ROMAN EMPIRE.

PATRICK WAS FAST asleep when it happened. He didn't hear the crunch of gravel as a band of stealthy figures dropped over the low stone walls. He didn't notice the shadows flickering across the moonlit window as the raiders crept past. He slept blissfully on until the screams began.

"Pirates! Run!"

He was suddenly awake and sitting up in bed. "What is going on?" he thought, shaking the sleep out of his head.

"Please don't hurt me!" cried a child's voice.

He ran to the door. A band of raiders was chasing the screaming farm slaves across the grass. One of the invaders hoisted a girl over his shoulder and ran towards the gate.

"Let her go!" An old man rushed from the stable with a shovel.

Swiftly, the barbarian drew a sword from a leather belt at his waist and blocked the swinging shovel. As he fell backwards, the old man kicked at the raider, causing him to stumble. He dropped the girl.

"You'll pay for that!" the invader screamed. He lurched to his feet, running his sword into the old man's belly. "Kill any who slow you down!" he cried to his men. "We only want the profitable ones!"

The girl scrambled toward the house. "Here!" Patrick whispered, darting out of the dark doorway and grabbing her hand. He shoved her inside, glancing over his shoulder. "Oh, no! He's spotted me!"

The raider's animal skin coat gleamed in the moonlight. He raised a razor-sharp sword and charged, his wild blond hair streaming out behind him. Patrick turned to run, but was struck from behind by a hard object. Instantly, everything went black.

When he opened his eyes again, he was in a dim room. A ceiling of animal hide stretched over him. Beneath him, the floor swayed. The air was close, and smelled of salt and body odor. "Am I on a ship?" he wondered, trying to remember how he got there. His head throbbed, and as he raised a hand to rub it, he felt the weight of iron and heard the clank of chains.

"You've been captured by pirates."

He turned in the direction of the voice. Next to him, against a wall, several men were shackled together. It looked like only one of them was awake.

"What did you say?"

"Irish barbarians. They raided several farms tonight. We'll be sold as slaves."

Slaves! Patrick stared at him in shock.

"You're lucky," said the man. "They kill the older ones, but a strong teenager like you was worth keeping."

"I should be glad I'm alive to suffer?"

"You should be glad you're alive."

A sound at the other end of the galley distracted him. A guard came through, and Patrick shut his eyes and pretended to be asleep. When the footsteps faded, he looked at his new companion again. A matted beard and long hair hid his age, but his eyes were alert. Above his left temple was a fading bruise and a crust of dried blood.

"How old are you, lad?" the man whispered.

"Fifteen."

"You're not a slave like the rest of us. Your parents are wealthy?"

Patrick hesitated. He wasn't sure if he should trust this man, but he was obviously in the same predicament. "Yes," he answered finally. "My father is a tax collector and a deacon in the church. My grandfather is a priest."

"You're from a Christian family?"

"Yes."

"A lot of good that did you."

"I beg your pardon?"

"How can you worship a god who allows your family to be captured by barbarians?"

"My parents were at our house in town," he replied, dropping his gaze. "They are safe. I was the only one at the farm, besides our slaves."

"But your god didn't protect you."

Patrick turned away and shut his eyes again. "I rejected my parents' religion. God is probably punishing me."

The man shifted and laid a shackled hand on Patrick's shoulder. "I didn't mean to discourage you, lad. Maybe your god will change his mind and let you go home."

"Maybe." Patrick's eyes had adjusted to the dimness, and now he could see dozens of young men and women in chains. He recognized some of his family's slaves among them.

They were at sea for several days. When the boat came into port, the captives were herded single-file across the gangplank in their chains. The Irishmen prodded them toward the auction house in the market. They were anxious to sell their merchandise and find a tavern.

A cold drizzle was falling, and Patrick sloshed through thick mud as they made their way up the hill toward the center of town. Patrick had heard of Ireland, but had never seen its shores. He had heard stories of giants roaming the land, of Irish savages who ate human flesh and worshiped strange gods. He shivered.

The pirates pushed him toward a wooden platform, surrounded by a rough, noisy crowd. They stared and pointed at him. He heard several languages, but recognized only Latin.

A round man in a colorful coat began to bargain with the auctioneer. Patrick couldn't tell what was being said, but he knew he was the subject. Within minutes, his chains were unlocked and he was shoved into the hands of a waiting escort.

"Where are we going?" Patrick asked. "What's happening?"

The men ignored his questions, dragging him toward a cart at the far end of the busy market. Hitched to a team of horses, the cart was piled high with barrels and crates. The big man was waiting for them, rain running in streams down his bushy mustache. He took Patrick's face in his hands, and turned it left and right, examining him like a doctor.

"Who are you?" Patrick demanded in Latin.

The man looked at him in surprise. "You speak Latin?"

"Yes."

He turned to his men. "This one is educated. Where did he come from?"

"He was on the boat with the others."

"Well, looks I got a deal." He rubbed his hands together. "What's your name?"

"Patrick, of Bannaventa Berniae."

"I am Miliucc, your master. You are my new shepherd. Serve me well, and you may one day be in charge of the cattle. Serve me poorly and you will be sold to the mines."

"I'm not a shepherd," Patrick said haughtily. "I'm a Roman nobleman, and I will soon be a tax collector like my father."

Miliucc laughed. "I'm your father now, and you better be worth the price I just paid for you." He gestured to one of his men. "Chain him to the cart."

The journey was grueling. Shackled behind the cart in the rain, Patrick tried to keep pace with the horses. The Irishmen stopped twice a day to feed and water the animals, and during those brief rests he sank gratefully into the mud and devoured the hard biscuits they gave him. "My family must think I'm dead," he despaired. "No, don't give up. Try to memorize the trail so you can escape later."

But every day was the same, and he lost track of all the twists and turns. The muddy road ran for miles along the coast and then wound through the forest. When they finally cleared the trees, the countryside rolled out before him in every shade of green. Even under the gloomy skies, the hills glowed like emeralds.

In the distance, the Irish homestead stood waiting for Miliucc's return. It was much smaller than Patrick's villa, and circled with a fence of sharpened wooden stakes, but it had the familiar smell of farm animals. The approach of the cart scattered a flock of sheep grazing near the door. Patrick saw that the house was made of twigs plastered with mud, and covered with a cone-shaped roof of reeds.

They removed his chains. At Miliucc's hail, a slave appeared.

"Make sure young Patrick here is given a proper explanation of his duties." He went into the house.

"I'm Victoricus. Welcome to Foclut." He was tall and muscular, and dressed in a wool tunic and trousers. Patrick guessed that he was in his thirties.

"This way," he said. They passed a garden and circled the house. "You will be tending those sheep," he said, pointing out at the hills.

In the fading daylight, a man was herding a flock toward the gate.

Some distance behind the main house was a hut. "When you are on the farm at night you will sleep in here," he said, opening the door. Inside were small alcoves with straw sleeping mats. Several slaves were working over a cooking fire. The close quarters produced a stench, but it was the only real shelter from the weather.

"If I'm not here, where will I be?" asked Patrick.

"In the fields with the flock. Come inside. We're about to have our evening meal, and no doubt Brendan will be glad to a have a new audience for his songs. He fancies himself a bard."

Victoricus introduced him to the others, and got him a bowl of stew. It was the first hot meal he had eaten since his last night at home.

That night Patrick slept soundly, exhausted from his journey. In his dreams, he felt the sunlight warming the pastures of his father's farm. He saw the blue sea, and the road into Bannaventa Berniae, and the second home his father kept in town. He followed the crisscrossing streets past orderly rows of houses to the bathhouse in the town square. Beyond it was the temple of Mithras, and further down the road, the familiar church. He was drawn toward the simple building topped with a cross. As he came closer, the doors opened wide in welcome, and his grandfather stood before the congregation. The priest slowly looked up, his black eyes meeting Patrick's in a piercing stare. As he stretched out an arm, a rushing wind suddenly swept the boy away.

"No!" yelled Patrick, jerking from his mat in a sweat. Surrounded by snoring slaves, he pushed his way to the door and ran outside. In the stillness, he heard pigs and cattle beginning to rise with the early light. It would be his first day as a shepherd, as a captive slave.

"Forgive me, God," he prayed aloud, falling to his knees. "I should have listened to my grandfather's warnings. I never should have rejected your word."

He felt a hand on his shoulder. "Patrick," said Victoricus, "it's time to take the flock out to pasture. Come inside for a slice of bread before you go."

As the seasons passed, Patrick took over the full responsibility of caring for the sheep. Every day for six years, he herded his flock over the mountains. In the summer he fought the rain. In the winter, with only a sheepskin coat and a wool blanket, he fought the snow and frost. At times he felt like his limbs would fall off. He longed to escape and return to Britain, but Miliucc frequently reminded him that runaway slaves were always caught. The punishment was severe.

He started each day with prayer before going out to pasture with the sheep. In the fields, he prayed as he worked. Some days he fasted and removed himself at meal times for more prayer. His unusual practices drew the attention of his fellow slaves.

He was kneeling by a tree early one morning when a young slave girl and her brother tiptoed closer to hear his prayers. They hoped to tell the others more about Patrick's odd religion.

"Father in heaven," prayed Patrick, "please forgive my sins of youth. Forgive me for offending you and for denying the salvation you so graciously provided. Deliver me from my enemies and bring me safely home to my family. Teach me how to declare your truth with joy. Show me how to live as Christ lived and to wait for that day when I will be forever with you, almighty Father. Amen."

He opened his eyes to see the children standing across from him.

"Why do you fast?" asked the girl.

Patrick smiled and rose. "Good morning, Eilidh. Hello, Eoin."

"Why do you fast, Patrick?" she insisted.

"I fast because I wish to return home," he said, walking toward the sheepfold. They followed him.

"Did someone offend you?" asked Eoin.

"What do you mean?"

"When someone fasts, they do it to shame the person who offended them."

"No, that's not what I'm doing. I fast for my God," said Patrick.

"Did he offend you?" asked Eilidh, wrinkling her forehead.

"No," said Patrick with a chuckle. "I offended him. You do ask a lot of questions."

"What did you do to offend him?"

"He sent his son to die for me but I rejected his gift of grace."

"Everyone thinks you're crazy," said Eilidh. "They call you Holy Boy."

Eoin gave his sister a nudge. "Eilidh! That's not nice," he whispered.

"I'm not crazy," Patrick insisted. "I believe in Jesus Christ and not the gods of the other slaves. They hope these gods will free them, but they are merely idols. There is only one God and only he can truly free us."

"Enough talking!" said Victoricus, joining them. "Time for work." The children ran toward the house.

Victoricus put his hand on Patrick's shoulder. "Patrick, I have allowed for your times of prayer and fasting, but please do not disrupt work. If you are late in getting the sheep out to pasture, Miliucc will have you whipped."

"I'm sorry," said Patrick. "I appreciate your kindness to me."

"We cannot fall behind in our work. But your stories of Christ are interesting. Perhaps tonight you will tell us a new one so we don't have to hear another of Brendan's woeful songs!"

But Patrick told no stories that night. Instead, he listened in amazement with his friends as one of the other slaves brought them news of far away: "Rome has fallen to Alaric of the Goths!"

"It makes little difference to us here."

"Yes, but who believed it was possible? The Romans have ruled for centuries."

"The world is changing," thought Patrick. "Everything changes, except my slavery and the slavery of the Irish people to their idols." He longed to return to his grandfather's church, and continued to pray for his escape.

On another night soon after, he had a vivid dream. When he awoke suddenly, he remembered only the words: "You have fasted well—soon you will be going home." It's only a dream, he thought. It means nothing.

But the next night, the voice returned: "Behold, your ship is ready!" Patrick again sprang up from his bed. "Is this God's way of saying I should go home?" He had long prayed for direction. "But if I leave, I'll be a fugitive, and I probably won't make it home. What if it was just a dream?"

He couldn't shake the feeling that God was telling him it was time to leave. He wrapped his tattered blanket around his shoulders, snuck out of the hut, and headed for the mountains. In the darkness he prayed, "Lord God, if I am to make it home, please supply my needs and keep me safe."

He was familiar with the mountain paths from wandering there with his sheep. But as the sun rose, he reached the forest and tried to find the road he had taken six years earlier.

He had heard tales of the druids and their human sacrifices, of the perils of being caught trespassing on the land of fierce local kings. "If I'm caught, I will be returned to Miliucc and punished. I must stay clear of the paths and towns."

Avoiding well traveled areas, he covered a few miles a day. He trudged through forests and swam across rivers. He ate whatever he could catch and slept on the ground rolled in his blanket. After many days, he arrived at the port where he had started, nearly a hundred and eighty-five miles from Miliucc's farm.

He sat in the shadow of a boat on the docks and observed the activity there. He had come so far, but he was still in danger. "If I approach the wrong captain, he'll turn me in," he reminded himself. He watched the ships for hours before making his choice.

The captain was giving directions to his crew. "My mother fares better than you do!" he shouted. "Britain isn't going to wait for this cargo, so get this boat moving!" When he turned back toward the dock, Patrick was standing behind him. He peered at him suspiciously. "What do you want?"

"Sir, I'd like to join your crew," Patrick said. "I'll work for my passage."

"Get out of here," replied the captain, turning away.

What now, Lord? he prayed.

"Wait!" called a sailor. "Captain, we're short on crew this time. We could use the extra hands."

The captain gave him a second look. He took in the weather-beaten face, the well-knit shoulders, the hands calloused with labor. "Get aboard," he finally growled. "See the mate for orders and don't cause me any trouble."

"Yes, sir. Thank you."

The captain strode away, and Patrick hurried to find the first mate.

They had been at sea for three days. A vicious storm battered the boat until the crew feared she would sink. "We've sighted land, but we'll never make it along the coast to port in this wind," a sailor told Patrick. "We have to ground her here."

Patrick helped row the sinking boat to shore and unload the cargo. "It's going to be a long walk," the captain grumbled.

"It can't compare to the miles I've already come," Patrick thought.

But they were far short of their destination. To pass the time as they traveled, the crew told stories, made bets, and argued. When they spoke of their gods, Patrick told them about Christ. They laughed.

After almost three weeks of hauling their cargo across the deserted land, the crew ran out of food.

"Well, Holy Boy, now what?" mocked the captain. "We're starving to death. If your god is so powerful, ask him for some food!"

"I already have," he replied. "Turn your heart to the Lord, Captain, because today he is going to send food right into your path." He continued to pray silently as they trudged along.

There was a shout from some of the crew who had gone on ahead. "Pigs, captain! Fat, beautiful, wild pigs!"

The sailors scurried after the pigs, laughing at each other's efforts to capture the grunting animals. The captain looked at Patrick in disbelief.

"Nothing is impossible for my God," Patrick said with a smile.

That night they feasted on roast pig and slept with full bellies. In the morning, they continued on their way with raised spirits. The weather stayed clear, and on the dry ground they made better time. Ten days later, just as they were running out of food again, they came upon a British settlement along the coast. Safe at last! Patrick sank to his knees in tears and thanked God.

After saying good-bye to the crew, he continued to Bannaventa Berniae. As the stone walls of the family villa came into view, he paused on the road and watched the slaves working in the fields. "I'll never think of slaves the same way again," he thought, looking down at his rough hands. He was now twenty-two, thin from lack of food but strong from work, with an untamed beard and long hair. His woolen trousers and tunic were just tattered, filthy rags. "I wonder if they'll even recognize me."

He drew near the house he'd seen so often in his dreams. As

his excitement grew, he began to run. A woman bent over in the vegetable patch looked up at him, startled. She stared for only a moment, and then, dropping an apron full of carrots, ran for the gate.

"Patrick?"

"Mother!"

He threw his arms around her and held her as she sobbed.

"Patrick's back!" cried the slaves, running for the house. "He's alive!"

Patrick's father came out of the barn, wiping his hands on his sleeves. His jaw fell when he saw Patrick. "Son? Son!" He covered the distance in only a moment, drawing the young man into a tight embrace.

With his father's arm around him and his mother covering his face with kisses, Patrick returned home. They sent a slave into town to announce the astonishing news and bring back Patrick's grandfather.

That night, in his father's small bathhouse, he had his first hot bath in six years. In fresh clothes, he joined a crowd of friends and family in the kitchen. While his mother filled his plate with roasted goose, he recounted his adventures. They sat breathlessly as he told them about his capture, his life as a slave, his escape, and his long, dangerous journey home.

"I could never have imagined all this would happen to me," he told them. "But in my hardship, I met Jesus. I have spent the last six years in prayer, and I'm sure God wants me to serve him in the church."

He looked at his grandfather, who rewarded him with a broad grin.

It was hard to adjust to his old life again. He often took walks along the coast, gazing out across the sea and thinking of the misty green hills that had almost killed him. "It's strange," he thought, "but I feel as though as I have left something behind."

One night soon after his return, he was sleeping in his old bedroom when he had another dream. Victoricus arrived from Ireland with a bundle of letters. Drawing one from the top of the pile, Patrick opened it and read, "Holy Boy, come walk among us!"

He awoke with a strange sorrow. "There are so many people there who worship idols, so many slaves who don't know Jesus. Someone must go to tell them."

"Patrick! They tried to kill you! They'll try again if you go back," his mother said when he told her of his decision.

"I know better than anyone how dangerous it is," he replied. "But I believe God is calling me to become a bishop and return to Ireland as a missionary."

"May the Almighty Father protect you," she whispered, kissing the top of his head and leaving it wet with her tears.

"He will, Mother. He has a job for me." Patrick set out for the church to begin his training. He was going back to Ireland.

Patrick returned to Ireland to bring the gospel to his former captors, and faced many more dangers. The Roman Empire never conquered Ireland, but, through Patrick, Christianity did. He died an old man, around the year 460.

BENEDICT: RENOUNCE YOURSELF AND FOLLOW CHRIST

529 AD. MONTE CASSINO, ITALY.

SHADING THEIR EYES with their hands, two men followed their companion's upturned gaze. The massive, rectangular walls rising against the clouds were the same sun-bleached gray as the mountain summit. Here and there, piles of stone lay where they had tumbled from the ancient fortifications, now covered with vines and shrubbery. The dark-haired man whistled. "So this is Monte Cassino. Our new home."

"It has seen better days," said their young companion, still pointing. "It will take a lot of work to turn that into a functioning monastery."

"God will supply our needs, Placid," replied the abbot. "Now that I see the location, it is clear why this fortress was a good defense for the city." He turned and looked out over the route they had climbed.

Behind him, along the twisting path, sprawled a caravan of monks and supply-laden donkeys. A dusty haze marked their progress up the mountainside. Sloping away toward the valley lay the simple buildings of Cassino, the citizen's sheep pens and cooking fires visible.

"It's not much further now," the older man said, facing the summit again and searching for secure footing in the stony ground. "Maurus, I'll go on and look for a safe area to set up for the night. Direct the brothers to follow. Tomorrow, we rebuild." He scrambled up the path.

"And Benedict founds another monastery," Maurus told Placid, urging the caravan forward.

For days, the monks had traveled southwest from Subiaco, trudging in silence alongside their donkeys. When they arrived in Cassino in their coarse, soiled tunics, the residents welcomed them with open curiosity. Over fresh-baked bread, Benedict informed the residents that Senator Tertullus had given him the crumbling fortress at the top of the mountain for the establishment of a monastery.

When the sun rose that morning, they began to ascend the slope. A number of the townspeople traveled with them. It caused quite a stir when they unexpectedly came upon a sacred grove, a circle of trees surrounding a pagan altar.

"Idols!" cried Benedict in disgust.

"There are many such groves," said one of the townspeople. "The mountain is the home of our gods."

"Our enemy is strong in this town," said Maurus, frowning.

"Not anymore," Benedict declared. "This land now belongs to the monastery, by grant of Tertullus. We will search out every one of these idols and tear them down."

But first, they needed to rebuild the massive fortress and plant crops to sustain their new community.

As the monks led their donkeys toward the summit, Benedict wandered carefully through the musty chambers of the old refuge.

"These cells will be fine for sleeping once the walls are patched," he thought, "and down this corridor is an area that must have once been used as a kitchen. Now I just need to locate a good place for prayer."

He came upon an open courtyard. The ground was covered with broken paving stones choked by tufts of grass. Opposite where he stood, a statue of a young man poised with bow and arrow led into a pillared structure. Benedict noticed an inscription, but it was mottled with moss and he had to concentrate to make out the words: To the mighty Apollo. It was a pagan temple, and he could tell from the wilted flowers at Apollo's feet that it was still used on occasion.

"The locals must come here to worship their false god," he thought. "I could tear the temple down, but it appears to be in good condition, and we'll need a chapel." He sat down on the ground and made a mental note to have the men start their renovations here.

"Tertullus has done us a great service," he thought. "These ancient walls overlooking the town are a perfect place for a community of quiet contemplation and prayer." Over the last fifteen years, he had built twelve monasteries in Subiaco, so he knew what he was doing. Still, it was hard to believe he was doing this, considering his former life.

Like all educated people, he came from a wealthy family, and as a child never wanted for anything. His parents taught him to love Christ, and when they sent him to Rome to go to school, he was appalled at the corruption he saw in the church. He did not want to be part of it, but he wasn't sure how to control his sinful desires. "I must get away from temptations," he told himself, so he gave away his possessions and fled Rome.

"Perhaps if I live by myself with no one else to influence me and no material comforts to love, then I will no longer be tempted. I will trust God to supply my needs."

Several miles east of Rome, near Subiaco, he met a monk named Romanus. "Please tell me where I might find solitary shelter," he asked.

"I can take you to my monastery," Romanus offered.

"No, no, I must be by myself. Perhaps there is a barn or an abandoned house?"

Romanus pointed to a drop-off, away from the road. "There are no houses in the area, but there is a cave in the side of that cliff," he said. "It is not easy to get to, and there is no food."

"God will take care of me. Thank you for your help."

He scaled the cliff face and found the opening. It was dark and damp. "Perfect. Alone here, I will have no temptations."

But he soon discovered that though his hands were empty, he had brought many temptations with him. He was lonely and hungry, and at night he was cold with only his filthy sheepskin cloak. He was miserable, and considered going back to Rome.

"Devil!" he cried out, swatting at his invisible enemy as though he were a fly. He had plenty of time to argue with the enemy, and there was no one else to talk to. "Take leave of me, Satan," he shouted at the cave's entrance. "I will not be tempted to leave my refuge."

"The things of this world mean nothing to me," he mumbled, retreating back into his cave. "What is eternal, Devil—that is what lasts." He stumbled on a rock in the darkness.

"Benedict!" The unexpected sound echoed inside the cavern, followed by the jingle of a bell. "Benedict, are you in there?"

For a moment he wondered if the devil had decided to answer him. Then he saw a bundle dangling from a rope at the mouth of the cave. A breeze caught the bundle as he reached for it and smashed it against the rock wall, shattering the little bell. The knot let loose, and Benedict snatched up the bundle before it fell and tore it open.

Several crusts of bread were tied into a scrap of fabric.

"Romanus?" He stepped out onto the ledge and looked up.

"Hello, Benedict!" the monk said, peering over the edge of the drop-off. "I thought you might be hungry enough by now to share my bread."

"The Devil tried to take it from me, but I have it now!"

Romanus pulled up the rope and smiled. "It would be easier if you joined us at the abbey."

"Not today. The world is too tempting for me. But thank you for the food." He waved good-bye and sat down at the mouth of the cave. Chewing deliberately, he tried not to think about how good the bread tasted.

Romanus came back the next day, and most days after that. In the shadows of the evening, when the sun's heat retreated, Benedict would stroll to the edge of his cave and look out in the distance at the ruins of Emperor Nero's palace. When he was thirsty, he made his way down to the river for water, but it was the only reason he left the cave. Only when he received some dignified visitors one day did he consider leaving his cave permanently.

"You are known as a man of discipline," said two noblemen, Equitus and Tertullus. "We want you to become an abbot and raise our sons Maurus and Placid to serve God. We will provide you with land and supplies to build a monastery."

Benedict thought about their proposal. "I have removed myself as far from temptation as possible, but am I serving God here? Perhaps training others to resist the cares of the world is a better use of my time."

He accepted their offer.

When he had founded the first abbey, more young men arrived to be trained. He started another abbey, then another. Now the first boys he had trained were men, and they had come with him to the mountain of Cassino to help him start yet another abbey.

"Make this a community that honors you, Father," he said aloud.

Maurus and Placid found him on his knees in prayer in the neglected courtyard. "The caravan is here, Abbot," Placid said. "Where should we begin to unload the supplies?"

He smiled at them and got to his feet. "This way, brothers."

Benedict and the monks moved into the fortress, laboring day after day to make it their home. They hauled stone, pulled weeds, repaired the roofs, cleared rubbish, and planted crops. Several times a day they paused from their work to pray together and read Scripture aloud. Soon they had restored the kitchen, individual sleeping cells, and a large chamber to use as a library and workroom for copying books.

As soon as they had settled in, they searched the mountainside for the sacred groves. The pagan altars were overturned. "The gods are no longer on the mountain," the townspeople murmured.

Benedict began to spend his afternoons in town, explaining why they had removed the idols and telling them about the salvation offered by the true God's son, Jesus. "Renounce your false gods and your sinful heart!" he urged them. "Renounce yourself and follow Christ."

One evening, Benedict retreated to his tiny cell to pray. His hands were calloused with work, his muscles sore from the heavy labor. He knelt on the stone floor, glad for an hour to spend with his God.

"Our Father," he prayed aloud. "You are holy and faithful. Your servants are weak, but you have blessed our work. You have supplied all of our needs, granting us the honor of copying Bibles, preserving the writings of your saints, and feeding the poor of this land. Thank you for moving the hearts of the people of Monte Cassino to turn from their idols. Keep us from sin. Give me and my brothers the strength to resist the world. Make this monastery a beacon of your gospel, an example of godliness to Monte Cassino and to people everywhere."

When he looked up from his prayer, he found Maurus standing at his door.

"I didn't want to disturb you, Abbot," Maurus said. "Placid said you wished to see me."

"Yes, come in, brother." He offered the young man a wooden chair, the only furniture in the room besides a narrow bed and a small writing desk. "How long have we worked together?"

Maurus smiled. "Over sixteen years, and each has been an adventure."

"Do you remember the day we met?"

"I was only a child. Placid was even younger."

"When your fathers came to me in my cave all those years ago, I wasn't sure I should respond to their request," Benedict said. "I had spent very little time in a monastery and I wanted only a life of solitude."

"But God gave you a grand calling! With the blessings of our fathers, you raised us and dozens of sons from other important families who wanted to support the work of the gospel."

"I consider it an honor to have founded those monasteries in Subiaco. Though our supporters outweighed our enemies, it was hard work. Remember the difficulties we faced because of Bishop Florentius? Here, we have few supporters, and our opposition to the local idols has already created enemies."

"Florentius was jealous," said Maurus. "He tried to poison you and discredit you. God showed him his error when his balcony collapsed and killed him."

"We must pray that God will show mercy on our enemies and teach them his truth," Benedict said, taking a small book from his desk. "When they learn how much he has done for them, they will join us in worship."

"Perhaps God will perform a great work to prove to everyone that we are his messengers."

"Perhaps he will. Either way, we will be faithful to him." He stood. "Now, let me show you something."

Benedict handed him the book. The pages were covered with the abbot's careful handwriting.

"What is this?"

"Some monasteries have a set of written rules to guide the monks," said Benedict. "When I started out in that cave so many years ago, I didn't have the benefit of rules. I was not accountable to anyone. But here, I want the brothers to have something to guide them when I'm gone, a rule to guard them from the distractions of the world."

Maurus glanced through the pages. "It looks like there are a lot of rules here."

"They remind us to deny ourselves and live in obedience to God's Word," said Benedict. "For example, the abbot is not to show favoritism. He is to teach the Bible to the brothers in both word and deed."

"You mean the abbot must live by the same rules as the brothers."

"Exactly." Benedict nodded. "The brothers are to renounce themselves and follow Christ. They must never repay a bad deed with another. To keep them from gossiping and grumbling against God, they are to practice silence unless they have permission to speak. Their days should begin with prayer and singing praises to God."

"Yes, I see. And you say that prayers should not be an opportunity for pride, so the brothers should keep their prayers short."

"Some people like to hear their own voices," Benedict explained. "I've also included rules to keep them from eating too much, or becoming vain by wearing fancy clothes."

"Vanity is one of the Devil's greatest tools," agreed Maurus.

"My rule will seem harsh to some, but it will build spiritual fences around the brothers, helping them keep out the bad influences in the world."

"Benedict's Rule of Order," said Maurus. "We will make copies of this for all the monasteries in Subiaco." He left the room, eagerly reading the manuscript.

Benedict blew out his candle and climbed, exhausted, onto the hard bed frame covered with straw. "Perhaps this bed is too much of a luxury," he wondered as he fell asleep.

With the obvious changes at Monte Cassino, stories about the monastery spread to neighboring towns. People became curious about Benedict and his quiet community. Visitors began to drop in to observe their work.

It was late morning, and several of the monks were hoeing a patch of cabbages in silence. Within the monastery walls they had planted a large garden. Neat rows of herbs, onions, and various vegetables provided enough food for the monks and the poorest residents of Cassino.

As the sun climbed higher in the sky, the temperature in the garden rose with it. Benedict wiped the sweat off his brow and took a last swipe at a stubborn vine that threatened to overpower the tight row of cabbages. "It is time for the noon meal," he announced quietly.

The monks shouldered their tools and filed out of the garden. Taking up the rear, the abbot followed them towards the kitchen, pausing at the entrance to the courtyard. He smiled with approval on the progress they had made.

The overgrown weeds had been cleared away, revealing a small fountain. Now that it had been repaired, a stream of water bubbled cheerfully into the basin. He had scrubbed the large paving stones that covered the ground himself, removing years of dirt and mildew. Maurus and Placid had torn down the statue of Apollo. "I suspect they had a bit too much fun doing that," Benedict thought. "But they did work hard to clean up the mess." Where the statue had stood was now a tidy bed of yellow blossoms.

The most impressive change was the temple. Once the pillars had been polished, the inscription to Apollo rubbed out, and the pagan altar carried away, they had dedicated the new chapel to Saint John the Baptist. Now the brothers gathered there for daily prayers.

Turning back toward the kitchen, he heard hurried footsteps along the stones. "The monks never run. Is something wrong?" He looked back sharply.

Maurus stopped breathlessly before the abbot.

"What is the matter, brother?" Benedict asked.

"The barbarians, Abbot! An army has stopped at the foot of the mountain, and a band of barbarians is marching toward the abbey."

"Perhaps they are men of God come to worship with us."

Maurus stared at him. "They're barbarians."

"Find out what they want."

"Yes, Abbot."

Before Maurus reached the other side of the square, Placid arrived with a tall, broad-shouldered man. He was obviously not from Italy.

"He has a message for you, Abbot," Placid announced.

The man had a strong accent. "King Totila of the Goths wishes an audience with Benedict of Nursia."

"The king is welcome," replied Benedict. "I will see him here. But we are a quiet community. He must not bring his army."

The messenger gave him a slight nod and marched out.

Benedict sat down on a stone bench facing the flower bed. Maurus and Placid stood on either side and gave each other a cautious glance.

A man entered the courtyard, accompanied by three bodyguards. Several attendants followed, carrying a golden spear and a plumed helmet. Benedict looked at the leather riding boots, at the linen garments fixed with a jeweled clasp, at the long, blond curls. "Son," he said calmly. "Lay aside the robes you are wearing. They do not belong to you."

The king dropped his gaze and backed away, taking his attendants with him.

Maurus and Placed looked at one another in astonishment.

The abbot waited patiently on the bench. In a few moments, another man in a plain tunic entered alone, and when he saw Benedict, he fell to the ground.

"Rise, friend," Benedict called to him.

He remained where he was, with his face pressed against the stones.

Benedict stood and went to him, putting a gentle hand on his shoulder. "Please, do not kneel."

"You are a prophet as they said!" He rose to his knees and regarded Benedict with sharp blue eyes. "I am Totila, King of the Goths."

"Who told you I am a prophet?"

"The people of Italy speak of your deeds and claim you have performed miracles in Monte Cassino."

"Who is the young man who tried to deceive me?"

"Riggo is my sword-bearer. I gave him my robes and my attendants to see if you would accept him as the king. It was a test to see if you are really a man of God, but now I see I was mocking you."

"Why are you here?"

"Emperor Justinian tried to win back Rome from the Goths. I am on my way to conquer the empire once and for all."

Benedict drew himself to his full height. "You, Totila, have been the cause of many evils in this land. Your crimes have long gone unpunished. Put an end to your wickedness! God may let you conquer Rome, but I cannot imagine that with all the blood on your hands you will live more than ten more years."

The king stared at him with an open mouth. "Please, Abbot," he cried. "Give me a blessing!"

"The only blessing I can give you is to tell you to turn from your ways, or your sins will find you out."

Totila held Benedict's gaze for a moment. Then he bowed his head, and backed away. Pausing at the fountain, he glanced back, and with a nod to the abbot, he left. They soon heard the pounding hoofbeats of many horses as the king and his attendants galloped down the mountainside.

"If our service here brings a feared warrior like Totila to hear about God, then we have brought glory to our Savior," Benedict declared. "We must continue to battle our greater enemy, Satan, and overcome his temptations."

Maurus and Placid fell in line behind him as they headed back toward the kitchen. But they were stopped by another monk who had a small, lean boy in tow. Benedict gave the child a friendly smile. "Hello, young man. Have you come up from Cassino for food?"

"Please, sir," the child replied. "I was playing on the mountain when the barbarians arrived. I have heard you talk in town of Jesus, and now I see that even Totila listens to you."

"Jesus cares for the mighty as well as the weak, Son."

"Yes, sir. Please, may I stay with you here and learn more about Jesus?"

The abbot grinned at Maurus and Placid, and tenderly reached for the boy's hand. "I will talk to your father about that this evening," he promised. "Right now, let's get you some dinner."

Benedict continued to preach to the townspeople and teach his Rule of Order to the monks of his monastery. Today, the Benedictine order of monks still lives by the Rule. Benedict died in 547.

In 549, King Totila re-captured Rome for the Goths, and died three years later. The great Roman Empire had finally come to an end, but Christianity flourished.

⊕THER EARLY CHRISTIANS

AMONG THE EARLY Christians who are important to church history, there are many who left us little information about their lives. But these Christians are important to the church because of what they wrote about the Bible. Here is an introduction to a few of these ancient fathers.

Irenaeus was born in Smyrna around 115 and was a student of the martyr Polycarp. He taught in Rome before he became bishop of Lyon in southern Gaul (France). When Bishop Eleutherius succeeded Victor in Rome in 189, there was a dispute over the date of Easter. The church in Rome tried to force the churches in Asia Minor to accept their date for celebrating Jesus' resurrection. Irenaeus wrote a letter to Eleutherius reprimanding him for his actions. He is best known for his many books written against the heresy called Gnosticism. His books give us a glimpse into the beliefs of the early church.

Tertullian was a North African writer and lawyer, born around 160. He was probably the son of a Roman centurion. He became a Christian as an adult and was made a presbyter of the church. A very educated man, he wrote many books on theology and defenses against heretics. He also wrote a book to his wife, urging her not to remarry if he died, but to instead devote herself to serving Christ as a widow. Much of Tertullian's lifetime was spent in the church of Carthage. Later, he joined a group called the Montanists, who were eventually considered heretics. But his books continued to be popular among Christians. Many of our beliefs about the Trinity are influenced by his writings.

Clement of Alexandria was a teacher who combined Christian principles and Greek philosophy. Born around 160, his full name was Titus Flavius Clemens Alexandrinus. Known as Clement, he founded a school in Alexandria (Egypt). His most famous student was Origen, who also became a teacher in Alexandria. Under the persecution of Septimius Severus, Clement fled Alexandria and went to Cappadocia, leaving the school in Origen's care. He died in 215.

Hipploytus was an educated man, born around 170, who became a theologian in Rome. He wrote books against false teachings, on the book of Daniel, and on the second coming of Christ. He often referred to the teachings of Irenaeus. His opposition to Zephyrinus, the bishop of Rome, started a controversy. Emperor Maximinus Thrax exiled him to Sardinia in 235, and he was martyred about a year later.

Eusebius of Caesarea was the first major historian of the ancient church. Without his writings, we would know far less about early Christianity. He was born around 260, and in Caesarea he studied under Pamphilus, a student of Origen. After Pamphilus died, Eusebius became the bishop of Caesarea and attended the famous Council of Nicea in 325. He died around 339.

Hilary of Poitiers was the great defender of the Trinity in the west, just as Athanasius was the great defender of the Trinity in the east. Hilary was born in Poitiers (France) around 315. As an adult, he became a Christian and was elected as bishop of Poitiers in 353. In 355, when Emperor Constantius II tried to force the orthodox Christians to accept the Arian teaching and denounce Athanasius, Hilary refused. As punishment, he was exiled to the east, where he studied the teachings of the Council of Nicea and wrote books on the Trinity. But the emperor decided that Hilary was causing too much trouble in exile, so in 360 he was sent home. He continued to fight against Arianism until his death in 367.

Author Information

Mindy and Brandon Withrow are writers and active bloggers who have lived most recently in Philadelphia, Pennsylvania and Birmingham, Alabama. Brandon is adjunct professor of church history at Beeson Divinity School. They are both graduates of the Moody Bible Institute in Chicago; Brandon is also a graduate of Trinity Evangelical Divinity School and has a PhD in Historical Theology from Westminster Theological Seminary. One of their favorite activities is reading to their nieces and nephews.

WHERE WE GOT OUR INFORMATION

Brown, Peter. *Augustine of Hippo: A Biography*. Los Angeles: University of California Press, 1969.

Christian History magazine, select articles. Issues 37 and 80.

Comfort, Philip Wesley, editor. *The Origin of the Bible*. Wheaton, IL: Tyndale House, 1992.

Crouzel, Henry. *Origen*, Translated by A. S. Worrall. San Francisco: Harper and Row, 1989.

Deferrari, Roy Joseph, general editor. *The Fathers of the Church: A New Translation*, Vols. 15, 22, 39, 51. Washington, D.C.: The Catholic University of America Press, 1952, 1959, 1953, 1964.

Ewert, David. *A General Introduction to the Bible: From Ancient Tablets to Modern Translations*. Grand Rapids: Academie Books, 1983.

Freeman, Philip. *St. Patrick of Ireland: A Biography*. New York: Simon and Schuster, 2004.

Gonzalez, Justo L. *The Story of Christianity*. 2 Vols. New York, NY: HarperCollins, 1984, 1985.

Grant, Michael. *Constantine the Great: The Man and His Times*. New York: Charles Scribner's Son, 1993.

Hinchliff, Peter. *Cyprian of Carthage and the Unity of the Christian Church*. London: Geoffrey Chapman Publishers, 1974.

Kelly, J.N.D. *Jerome: His Life, Writings, and Controversies*. London: Duckworth, 1975.

Kelly, J.N.D. *Golden Mouth: The Story of John Chrysostom—Ascetic, Preacher, Bishop*. New York: Cornell University Press, 1995.

Kousoulas, D.G. *The Life and Times of Constantine the Great: The First Christian Emperor*. Second Edition. Bethesda, MD: Provost Books, 2003.

Maynard, Theodore. *Saint Benedict and His Monks*. London: Staples Press Limited, 1954.

McGuckin, John A. *St. Gregory of Nazianzus: An Intellectual Biography*. Crestwood, NY: St. Vladimir's Seminary Press, 2001.

McLynn, Neil B. *Ambrose of Milan: Church and Court in a Christian Capital*. Berkley, CA: University of California Press, 1994.

Peterson, Susan Lynn. *Timeline Charts of the Western Church*. Grand Rapids: Zondervan, 1999.

Ramsay, William M. *St. Paul: The Traveller and Roman Citizen*. Revised by Mark Wilson. Grand Rapids, MI: Kregel, 2001.

Roberts, Alexander. *The Ante-Nicene Fathers: Translations of the Writings of the Fathers Down to AD 325*. 10 vols. Grand Rapids: Eerdmans, 1969-1973.

Rousseau, Philip. *Basil of Caesarea*. Berkley: University of California Press, 1994.

Schaff, Philip. *The History of the Christian Church*, Vols. 1-3. Grand Rapids: Eerdmans, 1910.

Schaff, Philip, ed. *A Select Library of Nicene and Post-Nicene Fathers of the Christian Church*. Second Series. 14 vols. Grand Rapids: Eerdmans, 1952-1957.

Veyne, Paul, ed. *A History of Private Life*, vol. 1, From Pagan Rome to Byzantium. Translated by Arthur Goldhammer. Cambridge, MA: Belknap Press, 1987.

Foclut

Rhine

Alps

Verona

Milan

ADRIATIC

Rome

Monte
Cassino

Hippo   Carthage

Thagaste

Mal

THE
WORLD
OF THE
ANCIENT
CHURCH

BLACK
SEA

Constantinople · · Nicodemia
· Nicea
· Caesarea

AEGEAN SEA

· Smyrna
· Antioch

Caesarea·
Bethlehem·

MEDITERRANEAN SEA

Alexandria·

Nile

227

TORCHBEARERS

Polycarp waited until the sound of marching footsteps faded away. The Praetorian guard were on the move – ready to pounce on Christians or any other 'revolutionaries' that they might find.

These are the days when the catacombs are the dark shadowy refuges of the Christians and the amphitheatre is the sound of death to the believer. Polycarp will be one of the church leaders called on to give his life for Christ and his Kingdom… and this is something he counts as an honour.

To gain the Crown of Fire he must be willing to suffer for Christ. But will his courage hold? Accompany Polycarp and his companions as they face up to the Roman enemy and pass on the legacy of truth. The golden chain around Polycarp's neck is a link to the past in more ways than one.

William Chad Newsom is a new writer with a flare for the dramatic. Included in the book are a time line and further facts about the early church.

ISBN: 978-1-84550-041-2

LIGHTKEEPERS

Ten boys who made a Difference
ISBN 978-1-85792-775-7
Ten girls who made a Difference
ISBN 978-1-85792-776-4
Ten boys who didn't Give In
ISBN 978-1-84550-035-1

The Lightkeepers series by Irene Howat is an excellent collection of short biographies on famous and dynamic Christians from history and the present day. Fact files, prayers and quizzes will make these books favourites for years to come.

Look out for characters such as Augustine; Monica of Hippo; Polycarp and Alban - all characters influential in the early church. As well as people like Joni Eareckson Tada, Corrie Ten Boom and Martin Luther.

Other titles in this series are: Ten boys who Changed the World; Ten girls who Changed the World; Ten boys who made History; Ten girls who made History; Ten girls who didn't Give In.

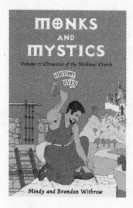

Monks and Mystics:
Chronicles of the Medieval Church
History Lives, Volume 2
ISBN: 978-1-84550-083-2

Read the stories of Gregory the Great, Boniface, Charlemagne, Constantine and Methodius, Vladimir, Anselm of Canterbury, Bernard of Clairvaux, Francis of Assisi, Thomas Aquinas, Catherine of Sienna, John Wyclif and John Hus. You can discover how the young Christian church moved on into another era of time to face the crusades and the spread of Islam as well as the beginnings of universities and the Reformation. Learn from their mistakes and errors but more importantly learn from their amazing strengths and gifts. Marvel at God's wonderful care of his people - the church - the Christian church.

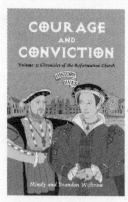

Courage and Conviction:
Chronicles of the Reformation Church
History Lives, Volume 3
ISBN: 978-1-84550-222-5

Read the stories of the reformers in the 16th and 17th centuries who changed the face of the Christian church forever. Meet the German monk, the French scholar, and the Scottish tutor who protested corruption in the church. Get to know the queens and explorers who risked everything for the freedom to worship according to their consciences. It was a time of war and upheaval, but also a time of promise and hope. From Erasmus and Luther to Katherine Parr and William Bradford, God used different personalities in different places to bring sweeping changes to church government and the way we worship. Learn from their mistakes and be encouraged by their amazing strengths and gifts.

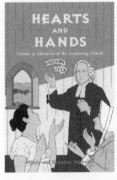

Hearts and Hands:
Chronicles of the Awakening Church
History Lives, Volume 4
ISBN: 978-1-84550-288-1

Read the stories of the gifted preachers and justice fighters who led the 1st & 2nd Great Awakenings in the 18th and 19th centuries. Meet the American preacher who started a national revival in his tiny church. Spend time with the wealthy English politician and the former American slave woman who helped abolish slavery in their countries. Get to know the missionaries who built lasting Christian communities in China, India, and Africa. From John Wesley and Jonathan Edwards to Elizabeth Fry and Harriet Beecher Stowe, God used the tender hearts and strong hands of his people to offer mercy to the world.

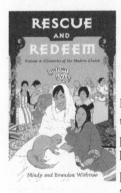

Rescue and Redeem,
Chronicles of the Modern Church
History Lives, Volume 5
ISBN: 978-1-84550-433-5

Read the stories of the Japanese samurai who traded his sword for a Bible and the Hawaiian princess whose faith strengthened her to defend her nation. Discover the German and Ugandan pastors who stood up to murderous dictators. Get to know the teacher in India who rescued child widows and the writer in Britain who created a world in a wardrobe. From Niijima Jo and Pandita Ramabai to Dietrich Bonhoeffer and Janani Luwum, they set out to rescue God's global people and redeem them to new life in Christ. Extra features throughout this book look deeper into issues such as modern Bible translation, living the Golden Rule, new developments in missions, and big moments in modern Christianity.

TWO SAMPLE EXTRACTS
FROM VOLUME 2

What was the Medieval Church?

THE WORD MEDIEVAL comes from two Latin words meaning "middle" and "age," so the medieval period of history is sometimes called the *Middle Ages*. The words remind us of castles and dragons, knights with enchanted swords, and queens in splendid garments. Historians usually identify the Middle Ages as the centuries between 600 and 1500 A.D. Christians who lived during these centuries are known as the *medieval church*.

Gregory the Great is considered one of the first leaders of the medieval church. But he would not have seen himself that way. Gregory did not wake up one morning in Rome and realize the church had entered a new age. He saw himself as carrying on the work of the early church fathers like Augustine and Benedict of Nursia. But as modern Christians look back on the past, we can see that Gregory's world was changing into a world quite different from that of the church fathers.

THE CHANGING STRUCTURE OF THE CHURCH

If the ancient church is the foundation of Christianity, the medieval church is the house built on that foundation. The early Christians were a scattered band, often hiding in fear of being persecuted for their beliefs. When Emperor Constantine declared Christianity a legal religion of the Roman Empire, the church began to organize into a formal institution. Public leaders were appointed, land was purchased, and beautiful buildings were constructed.

During New Testament times, Jerusalem was the most influential city. But by Gregory's time, Rome had earned that title. At first, the *bishop* of Rome was only one of many bishops overseeing the growing church. But as the church in Rome became more influential over the rest of the world, the bishop of Rome became the most influential church leader. He eventually became known as the *pope* (see "How the Pope Got His Name").

As their numbers grew, the church needed more leaders. Most cities needed multiple bishops to serve the large congregations of believers. So *archbishops* (like Anselm, Archbishop of Canterbury) were appointed to oversee all the bishops in a given region or *diocese*. The number of regions grew as the gospel spread into foreign lands. The church referred to itself as a *catholic* body, meaning "universal."

Many of the conflicts of the Middle Ages had to do with the struggle between the pope and the emperor (later the king) over who had ultimate authority. Pope Gregory commanded the armies of Rome. Pope Leo III crowned the neighboring King Charlemagne emperor after Charlemagne used his power to secure Leo's position as pope. Bernard of Clairvaux's preaching rallied thousands of soldiers to fight in the *Crusades* (see "What Were the Crusades?"). There was no clear distinction between the church and the state then, like most modern countries have today.

THE DEVELOPMENT OF MEDIEVAL TEACHINGS

While the structure of the church was changing, the teachings of the church were evolving, too. Medieval scholars studied in great detail the writings of the church fathers, and then wrote their own books. The more they discussed these teachings, the more complex these teachings became.

Some of their ideas are foreign to modern ears. Some are contrary to the gospel. It is often hard for modern Christians to remember that the people who developed these ideas were studying the Bible in the medieval world—a world very different from today. It would be centuries before the *Protestant Reformation*, a time beginning in the 1500s when many Christians protested some of these teachings and separated themselves from the established church. The medieval Christians did not see themselves as either *Protestant* or *Catholic* like we do today. They were simply members of a universal Christian body that was growing and changing in many ways.

Modern Protestants disagree with quite a few medieval ideas, but that does not mean that the men and women of the Middle Ages were always wrong or that they did not love God's Word. In fact, despite their differences, later Protestants admired many medieval thinkers like Bernard of Clairvaux and Thomas Aquinas. Like Christians of all eras, they made both positive and negative contributions to the church.

MONKS AND MYSTICS

The Middle Ages are dominated by the rise of the *monk* and the *mystic*. Gregory the Great founded Saint Andrew's monastery and became the first medieval pope. Two brothers named Constantine and Methodius left their monastery to become missionaries. Anselm was the *abbot* (a bishop in charge of a monastery) at Bec before he became Archbishop of Canterbury. Bernard of Clairvaux was not only the great preacher of the Crusades, but also the leader of the monastic group known as the Cistercian *order*.

Many of these men and women, like Catherine of Sienna, led a *mystical* life, one focused exclusively on prayer and the spiritual experience. These mystics concentrated on developing an intimate relationship with God.

Some of the people who had the greatest impact on the medieval church were not good role models. Emperor Charlemagne protected the pope and encouraged Christian education, but he also executed his enemies or forced them to be baptized. Prince Vladimir brought Christianity to Russia, but he was a ruthless conqueror who promoted

Christ for political reasons instead of a commitment to the gospel. Just as he does now, God used believers and unbelievers from all walks of life to spread the gospel during the Middle Ages.

MEDIEVAL BIOGRAPHIES: FACT OR FICTION

How do we know what life was like during the Middle Ages? Court records and letters that have survived the centuries tell us a lot. But the most common sources of information are *biographies* of church leaders. These "lives of the saints" were the most popular books of the day. Because they were written by people who admired the saints, the facts were often exaggerated to encourage readers to be more like these great men and women of God. This can make it difficult for us to know what really happened and what are just special effects added by the biographers. To uncover the truth, we have to read these biographies carefully, compare them with known facts, and accept the parts that seem most likely.

So be prepared! The world of the medieval church is full of heroes and villains, history and legend. In many ways it is different from our modern world. But the church of today, Catholic and Protestant, traces its roots back to the strange but fascinating Christians of the Middle Ages.

WHAT WERE THE CRUSADES?

CHRISTIANITY SPREAD RAPIDLY during the Middle Ages. So did an opposing religion called *Islam* (see the feature, "What is Islam?"). Christianity and Islam became popular for many reasons. Sometimes people accepted one of these religions because they truly believed in its teachings. Other times they accepted a particular religion because their homeland was conquered by rulers who were either Christian or Muslim.

By the year 1000, Muslims controlled most of the area in the Middle East known as the *Holy Land*. At first, Muslim rulers allowed Christians to go on *pilgrimages*, or devotional visits, to the city of Jerusalem. The *pilgrims* wanted to see where Jesus had taught and climb the hill where he had died. Muslim rulers allowed the Christian pilgrims to visit these sites in peace, as long as they paid taxes. But as political differences grew between Muslim and Christian rulers, the Muslims began to limit the pilgrims' visits to the Holy Land.

Christians believed that the Holy Land should be under their rule, since they were followers of Jesus. But Muslims and Christians traced their ancestors back to the biblical figure Abraham, so both believed they had rights to the land. Christian and Muslim rulers began to clash.

Since 1054, the Christian church had been divided between the east (Constantinople) and the west (Rome). (See the feature, "A Divided Church: The Great Schism of 1054.") After a series of clashes between the eastern church and their Muslim neighbors, Christians in the east asked the western church to join them in a *Crusade* to fight the Muslims.

The western church hoped that by working with their eastern brothers against a common threat, they would heal the division between the two sides of the church. So Pope Urban II (1042-1099) and a preacher named Peter the Hermit (1050-1115) called the people to war in 1096.

Thousands of men, women, and children volunteered to join the Crusade. Some did it because they believed Jerusalem belonged to Christians. Their battle cry became, "God wills it!" Others did it because the pope told them God would forgive all of their sins if they helped defeat the Muslims. And some were simply ambitious men seeking fame, power, and riches.

The *Crusaders* captured Jerusalem. The church soon established a military order called the *Knights Templar*. They took vows like monks, and dedicated their swords to protecting pilgrims and defending the Holy Land. The *Knights Hospitallers* were based in a hospital in Jerusalem, and vowed to care for the sick.

They maintained control of the city for nearly a century. But as they fought among themselves, they gradually lost their power. A key defense city, Edessa, fell to the Muslims in 1144.

So a Second Crusade was called, and again the people were stirred to action by a preacher. An abbot named Bernard of Clairvaux was one of many Christians who were convinced that God wanted the church to regain the Holy Land. His sermons inspired thousands of Crusaders.

There were Christians who opposed the Crusades. Anselm, Archbishop of Canterbury, objected to war. He argued that Christians should reason with Muslims, and convert them to Christianity instead of force them out of the Holy Land.

The Crusaders became even more power hungry. Like before, they fought against each other, and the Second Crusade was a complete failure. Thousands died before they ever reached Jerusalem.

But the Crusades continued. In 1189, a Third Crusade was led by Holy Roman Emperor Frederick Barbarossa (1123-1190), King Philip Augustus (1165-1223) of France, and King Richard "The Lion-Hearted" (1157-1199) of England. It was more successful than the previous attempt.

In 1202, the Fourth Crusade was called by Pope Innocent III (1160-1216), but instead of fighting against the Muslims, Crusaders from the west plundered the city of Constantinople. The eastern empire became weak, and was eventually conquered by Muslims in 1453.

Four more Crusades followed between the years of 1217 and 1270.

In the end, Jerusalem remained under Muslim control. The eastern and western churches became more divided than before. And the gospel of Christ had been polluted by violence. The Crusades became a sad and horrifying period of the history of the Christian church.

CHRISTIAN FOCUS PUBLICATIONS

Christian Focus | Christian Heritage | CF4K | Mentor

Christian Focus Publications publishes books for adults and children under its four main imprints: Christian Focus, CF4K, Mentor and Christian Heritage. Our books reflect that God's word is reliable and Jesus is the way to know him, and live for ever with him.

Our children's publication list includes a Sunday school curriculum that covers pre-school to early teens; puzzle and activity books. We also publish personal and family devotional titles, biographies and inspirational stories that children will love.

If you are looking for quality Bible teaching for children then we have an excellent range of Bible story and age specific theological books.

From pre-school to teenage fiction, we have it covered!

Find us at our web page:
www.christianfocus.com

CF4•K
Because you're never
too young to know Jesus